The Gospel of Barnabas

The Gospel of Barnabas

DAVID SOX

London
GEORGE ALLEN & UNWIN
Boston   Sydney

George Allen & Unwin (Publishers) Ltd,
40 Museum Street, London WC1A 1LU, UK

George Allen & Unwin (Publishers) Ltd,
Park Lane, Hemel Hempstead, Herts HP2 4TE, UK

George Allen & Unwin Australia Pty, Ltd,
8 Napier Street, North Sydney, NSW 2060, Australia

First published in 1984

ISBN 0 04 200044 0

Set in 10 on 11 point Plantin by V & M Graphics Ltd, Aylesbury, Bucks
and printed in Great Britain
by Billing and Sons Ltd, London and Worcester

For Frances Maeda and Benedict Groeschel, OFM. Cap., dear friends and colleagues in those bright early years of the ecumenical dialogue when we thought so much was possible . . .

Contents

Introduction

The exquisite library of Prince Eugene of Savoy is in the grand hall (*Prunksaal*) of the Hofburg, Vienna's massive palace-fortress of the Habsburgs. The Austrian royal library was established in the fourteenth century, and with the addition of the prince's collection in 1738, constituted one of the most important accumulations of manuscripts outside the Vatican. One of those manuscripts was the reason I went to the library in February of this year. Like many of Prince Eugene's books, the one I came to see is kept in a box container which was constructed to appear as a book and is ornamented with his coat of arms. Like most of the volumes, it bears little trace of being much used by the connoisseur. Unlike his other books, this one has been singled out as a literary fraud – and a most unusual one at that.

I was allowed to examine *The Gospel of Barnabas* in an adjoining room which has the appearance of a laboratory. There was the musty smell of old paper, and efficient attendants in white coats made certain the few visitors used pencils instead of ballpoint pens in writing their notes. Plastic covers were placed over the manuscripts while they were viewed. My first impression of Codex 2662 was of its small size and good condition; outside its 'box' it measures roughly six inches by five. The gospel is a thick quarto of 255 leaves bound in thin but stiff boards covered with blackish-green leather. The codex, with its steady and meticulous script, certainly did not appear the object of harsh polemical debate.

Today *The Gospel of Barnabas* is basically unknown in the West except as a footnote in the more comprehensive accounts of Islamic studies or New Testament apocrypha. In sections of the Muslim world, it is another matter: *Barnabas* has become a major polemical tool as a challenge to the authenticity of the Gospel tradition and the foundations of Christian theology. Christian spokesmen in Pakistan, India, Indonesia and Egypt have been made aware of its significance to Muslim polemicists – it is impossible for them to ignore it.

I first became aware of *Barnabas* while writing about the interest a Muslim sect, the Ahmadis, had shown in the Turin Shroud. The Ahmadis were impressed by the speculation of certain observers that the image on the relic might indicate that Jesus had survived death on the cross. Following that experience, I came across mentions of the gospel in a number of Muslim tracts and finally, and more importantly, in several serious analyses in academic journals. The influence of *Barnabas* appeared difficult to dismiss.

In part, this book is a study in polemics, the now unfashionable art of theological disputation. At one time, polemics was a recognised branch of theology devoted to the refutation of errors; now the word reeks of inquisitional tactics and heresy hunts of a bygone age. Its more respectable theological sister, apologetics, the defence of the faith on intellectual grounds, is also generally played down in the ecumenical climate of the modern Church, receiving little of the attention it once had on the curricula of theological colleges.

Many Christian priests and teachers exercising their ministry in Muslim countries (we used to call them missionaries!) are being forced to react to *The Gospel of Barnabas* because of its popular use by their Muslim counterparts. It seems to me that the realities they face – which more and more are being brought to the attention of the West – should be better known to the general reading public. Like it or not, the new vigour in Islam is making itself felt, and not only in political and economic areas. Islam and Christianity are both woefully ignorant of each other in many respects. In the aftermath of events in the Lebanon, Egypt and especially Iran, Christians still operate with rather medieval assessments of Islam, and Muslims see no value in better understanding a religion which theirs has overtaken.

The polemics surrounding *The Gospel of Barnabas* present a strong attack upon the very corner-stone of the Christian faith – Jesus' death and Resurrection – and the Church's authority to decide what scriptures are to be accepted as the revealed Word of God. The Dutch scholar Jan Slomp has taken a keen interest in *Barnabas*, but to other Western scholars the book remains so repugnant that they refuse to make any comment on it. Slomp is a noteworthy example of the Christian participant in the dialogue between Christians and Muslims who doggedly tries to keep it open and honest and is not blind to the more unpleasant aspects which

2

need to be aired. He believes in the continued importance of apologetics, which is still 'useful in clearing the ground for dialogue on the real issues at stake'.[1] It is this feeling which, in part, has led me to write this book. The dispute over *Barnabas* in many areas of the Muslim world clouds far more important issues which both Christians and Muslims need to come to grips with.

There are other reasons for an examination of the Vienna manuscript in a book aimed at the general reading public. A little digging reveals facets of the document which have gone basically unnoticed and present some fascinating possibilities. Just why was it written? I give a possible scenario for authorship which asks for future exploration into the murky scene of the Inquisition in Venice and the inscrutable figure of Sixtus V. I have a hunch there is more to the story than I was able to uncover.

In Chapters 5 and 6 problems are discussed which justify the need for a new approach in koranic studies in the West – and by a breed not afraid to cross swords with established authorities. I have found scholars in the field of Islamic studies, and even more so in that of Gnosticism – especially in my native America – to be remarkably unco-operative to any one outside their cliques. The koranic denial of the Crucifixion has fascinated a number of scholars, and the reader of *Barnabas* – if he survives the first two-thirds of its 222 chapters – is struck by the portrayal of Judas taking Jesus' place in the story of the Passion. *Barnabas* makes graphically clear what the Koran intimates, and its presentation is remarkably evocative of that given by early Muslim interpreters; in a dramatic sense, it takes us back to a polemic that is as old as the formation of Islam itself. Christian converts to Islam wrote in a remarkably similar manner.

Any serious discussion of *Barnabas* cannot avoid the larger issue of the respective ways in which Muslims and Christians handle their scriptures. Christians wearily accustomed to literary dissection and 'demythologizing' are suprised to discover that Muslims have never approached the Koran in this manner. This is a major difference between the two religions – fundamentalist Christianity excepted, of course! Attempts have been made by Western scholars to discover the roots and sources in the Koran. Some have been rather heavy-handed, as we shall see, and a number of scholars have given a Christian reading which, though irenical in intent, ends up being more offensive than the straightforward polemical attacks. Fundamentalist Christians continue the approach used by missionaries a century ago. Though they would deny it vehemently, Muslim and Christian fundamentalists have much in common. It is the fundamentalists of Judaism, Christianity and Islam who are experiencing the greatest success in winning new souls to their faiths in the Near East, Africa and the West. One is inclined to agree with Peter Nichols' comment in *The Pope's Divisions*: 'There will be a lot more religion in the future, much of it of an unpleasant kind.'[2]

Such terms as 'fundamentalist' and 'revival' are specifically American Christian in origin, and I, like many other writers, use them for want of better ones. In Western usage they have negative connotations and suggest a certain type of religiosity which is at times emotional and anti-intellectual; such a description is not always applicable to Muslim forms.

Simply as a historical curio, *The Gospel of Barnabas* presents great fascination: none of the 'modern apocrypha' has had a 'longer run', none has been approached with more polemical fury, and none possesses a more interesting historical background. With *Barnabas*, we enter a world of extraordinary individuals who have either been named in or involved with its pages: a pope who was formerly a father inquisitor in Venice; a Christian monk who turned Muslim and seems the most likely candidate for creating the spurious gospel; a Jewish expert who sees it as a link with early Jewish Christianity; a sheikh of Islam's most prestigious university who used it in his religious instruction to Muslim youth; the most listed writer in the Index of Prohibited Books from whose library in Amsterdam it surfaced in the eighteenth century; and the remarkable English clergyman and painter of 'tree-portraits' who with his wife translated the gospel over a four-year period 'in small hotel rooms, and far from books of reference'.

Arabic words are translated in a variety of fashions, and I have used a highly simplified form. I have also generally employed N. J. Dawood's usage of koranic terminology, and his translation of the Koran[3] because of its accessibility. I have followed popular spellings of 'Muhammad', 'Muslim' and 'Koran' but also continued sources' preferred spellings in quoted accounts. The designation *The Gospel of Barnabas* creates a certain problem. As we shall see, there are a few pages of a manuscript of *Barnabas* known through a particular writer, and the listing of a 'Gospel under the name of Barnabas' in ancient listings. I think it is clear that most of the time *Barnabas* is mentioned we are referring to the Italian manuscript; the title *Pseudo-Barnabas* appears to me somewhat

4

redundant. The *New English Bible* has been used except when otherwise noted.

I am indebted for the early stages of my interest in this work to two scholars. Firstly, Geoffrey Parrinder, professor of the comparative study of religions at the University of London and author of the invaluable *Jesus in the Qur'an*,[4] has patiently answered many inquiries and offered wise advice. I used his book extensively in Chapter 7, and I find his general approach both objective and timely. Secondly, Albert Hourani, Fellow of St. Antony's, Oxford, supplied me with useful material; also, his *Europe and the Middle East*[5] is an illuminating volume portraying Christian–Muslim relations and polemics over the centuries, and I refer to it often in Chapter 8.

Jan Slomp's critical analyses of *Barnabas* and wise words on the Christian–Muslim dialogue have been extremely useful, and I quote from his writings often and concur with his judgements in many respects. From 1964 to 1977 Dr Slomp was on the staff of the Christian Study Centre at Rawalpindi in Pakistan, and he is now in charge of a centre concerned with Muslims in Dutch society. Dr Slomp kindly offered many suggestions and improvements to my original manuscript.

Paul Grendler helped indirectly with the authorship problem discussed in Chapter 4 because his book *The Roman Inquisition and the Venetian Press, 1540–1604*[6] so comprehensively covers an area heretofore largely neglected by scholars writing in English. Professor Grendler offered some helpful insights in personal correspondence.

Despite the passage of time, the Raggs' volume on *The Gospel of Barnabas*[7] remains the authoritative work on the subject. It is a pity it is not more readily available, and I am appreciative that their publisher, the Clarendon Press, has given me permission to quote from their translation and findings. I also thank Hofrat University professor Dr Otto Mazal, director of the Osterreichische National-bibliothek in Vienna, for allowing me to examine the Italian manuscript and for the photographs of it he made available.

The director of the state archives in Venice, Dr Maria Francesca Tiepolo, allowed me to study the Holy Office file on Fra Marino and answered several important inquiries concerning it. I am sorry that the Franciscan centre in Venice was unable to uncover any more information concerning Fra Marino, and hope that a future writer might be able to discover more about him. I suspect there are a number of surprises which might be uncovered in time.

Good friends, the Rt Revd John A. T. Robinson and Dom Sylvester Houedard, have also given good insights and access to library materials. Gavin Ryan of Trinity College, Cambridge, kindly translated many portions of the Holy Office file from the Venetian archives; and I am also appreciative of the help of Jennifer Brooke of the American School in London and Roberto Partarrieu Ph.D. candidate at Georgetown University, in translating Spanish and Latin materials. Jerome Lawrence has given me permission to quote from *Inherit the Wind*, copyright 1955 by Jerome Lawrence and Robert E. Lee.

He that sides with a Party is adjudged to Hell by the Rest; and if he declares for none, he receives no milder Sentence from all.

John Toland, *Christianity Not Mysterious* (1696)

PART ONE
The Muslim Gospel of Barnabas

CHAPTER ONE

'This Strange Book'

Sixteenth Century

In the latter part of the sixteenth century, a Christian monk called Fra Marino had accidentally met with a writing of the Church father Irenaeus which spoke against St. Paul, alleging as his authority *The Gospel of Barnabas*. The monk became exceedingly desirous to find this gospel. One day he was with his friend, Pope Sixtus V, in the latter's private library. The pontiff fell asleep, and Fra Marino looked around for something to read: the first book he laid his hand on proved to be the very gospel he had been searching for. Overjoyed at the discovery, he hid his prize in the sleeve of his robe, and when the pope woke up the monk was gone – with the gospel.[8]

Fra Marino's gospel contained a complete history of Jesus Christ from his birth to his ascension; but, this one, unlike the four canonical Gospels, had Judas taking Jesus' place on the cross and the Lord foretelling: 'He it is whom the nations look for, to whom the secrets of God are so manifest that, when he cometh into the world, blessed shall they be that shall listen to his words ... He is Muhammad, the Messenger of God.'

Due to this experience Fra Marino became a convert to Islam. The gospel passed through different hands until it reached 'a person of great name and authority' in Amsterdam at the beginning of the eighteenth century. The celebrated connoisseur of books Prince Eugene of Savoy received the manuscript in 1738; and along with the rest of his library it found its way into the imperial library of Vienna (now the Osterreichische Nationalbibliothek), where it is still kept.

1924

Montague James's *The Apocryphal New Testament*, first issued in 1924, is described by its publisher as 'the first book to supply the English reader with a comprehensive view of the apocryphal literature connected with the New Testament'. James believes the existence of a 'Gospel under the name of Barnabas' to be 'most doubtful ... The extant book under that name (ed. Ragg, 1907) is in Italian, a forgery of the late fifteenth or sixteenth, by a renegade from Christianity to Islam.'[9]

1907

In 1907, Canon Lonsdale and Laura Ragg published their translation of the Vienna Codex number 2662, 'The True Gospel of Jesus according to the description of Barnabas his apostle'.[10] The Anglican missionary and scholar W.H. Temple Gairdner of Cairo was among the first to reply to the renewed Muslim interest in the work created by the translation. Writing only months after the Raggs' book appeared, he stated:

> The name (though not the contents) of this strange book had long been known in India, and was not unknown in Egypt, though it was but a name, it has been freely cited in these countries by interested parties, who showed their slender respect for truth by citing a book they had never seen or read, and almost certainly never would have read of but for a chance mention of it in Sale's *Introduction to the Qur'an* ... Now, however, an easily accessible edition has been given to the world, and there are many signs that the interest in this book is to be quickened, especially in the Moslem East. Translations are appearing both in India and Egypt, and the wildest talk is being indulged in as to the historical value of the book ... We believe that when honest men throughout the East know the contents of the book, they will assign its true historical value – which is exactly *nil*.[11]

1940s

Cairo's thousand-year-old al-Azhar University, the oldest in the Muslim world, has been a centre for religious higher education for Muslims from all over Africa and Asia, and its sheikhs are among the important spokesmen in Islam. In the 1940s one such sheikh, Professor Abu Zahra, used *The Gospel of Barnabas* in his religion classes and addressed an appeal to Christians: 'The most significant service to religion, and to humanity, would be for the Church to make an effort to study it [the Gospel of Barnabas] and to refute it, and to bring us the proofs on which it supports its refutation.'[12]

1966

14 June 1966, Shlomo Pines, a professor at the Hebrew University in Jerusalem, read a lecture entitled 'The Jewish Christians According to a New Source' which was later published by the Hebrew Academy of Sciences and Humanities, and the 'new source' created a stir among scholars around the world.[13] In the Excursus II to his lecture, Pines made reference to *The Gospel of Barnabas*, speculating about connections between it and Islamic or Ebionite texts. The Ebionites were a sect of Jewish Christians which flourished in the early centuries of the Christian era and stressed the binding character of the Mosaic law.

Pines felt that the Raggs' evaluation of the gospel was 'rather one-sided' and did not take into account 'the complexities of the work'. He noted that passages which 'appear to attest the Ebionite character of the gospel are quite numerous'. The scholar also presented a 'tenable hypothesis' that a gospel of *B. lam. s.* mentioned by the great eleventh-century scientist al-Biruni and related to the Ebionites' gospel 'may have been an early form of the Gospel of Barnabas'.

1976

In February 1976 Muammar el-Qaddafi hosted a Christian–Muslim dialogue in Tripoli. The official Vatican delegation found that the 700 participants had been allocated a large number of copies of the Koran and, as its 'Christian' counterpart, of *The Gospel of Barnabas*. No bibles were to be seen: no New Testament, not even a single portion of the canonical Gospels. The Vatican delegates protested and *Barnabas* was removed; but no bibles came to replace it. One of the Catholic participants said later that Qaddafi had asked him when the pope in Rome would at last produce the true Gospel, *Barnabas*, which he had been trying to hide for centuries.

1977

From 21 to 27 March 1977, a Second International Muslim–Chris-

11

tian Congress was held in Cordoba, which had served as the capital of Moorish Spain. Although 200 participants from twenty countries took part, most of the Arab delegations failed to come at the last moment because of the opposition of a sheikh of al-Azhar, who saw no useful purpose in the congress 'as long as the official Church did not change its attitude toward Islam and Muhammad'. According to the conference record, 'one of the moments of crisis' occurred following an address by Dr Maurice Borrmans on 'Christian Reaction to the Islamic Presentation of Jesus'. Among the 'strong reactions in the ensuing debate' were a series of questions presented by the Libyan Director of Religious Affairs, Professor Raja Sassi, on the Crucifixion and Paul's understanding of it, and on 'the importance of the Gospel of Barnabas'.[14]

1979

In the autumn of 1979, the Muslim Information Services of London issued Muhammad 'Ata ur-Rahim's *Jesus, A Prophet of Islam* with publicity which included advertisements in the city's underground. This book, published 'under the auspices of the Presidency of Shariah Courts and Islamic Affairs, Doha' was aimed at 'English language readers, especially those who profess the Christian faith'. The author's chief ammunition for arguing that the original Christian faith has been perverted by St. Paul and his theological successors was *The Gospel of Barnabas*, 'the only known surviving Gospel written by a disciple of Jesus, that is, by a man who spent most of his time in the actual company of Jesus during the three years in which he was delivering his message'. According to 'Ata ur-Rahim,

> The Gospel of Barnabas was accepted as a canonical gospel in the churches of Alexandria up until AD 325. It is known that it was being circulated in the first and second centuries after the birth of Jesus from the writings of Irenaeus ... who accused Paul of being responsible for the assimilation of the pagan Roman religion and Platonic philosophy into the original teaching of Jesus. He quoted extensively from the Gospel of Barnabas in supporting his views.[15]

1981

In 1981, the Lahore publishers Al-Kitab issued a new edition of

The Gospel of Barnabas. The cover asserted that *Barnabas* was 'the only Gospel which preached pure and unmixed monotheism' and that it had been

> dismissed by the Christians as apocrypha; not withstanding the fact that it was as old as Christianity itself and had remained prevalent in Spain, Egypt, and Syria etc. until it was banned in AD 325. It remained in oblivion for about 1500 years until it was discovered in the eighteenth century. But no sooner it was published than it was made to disappear. It is being published again. Barring a few interpolations about matters not religious (and even the canonical Gospels are not free of interpolations) we leave it to the reader to judge by going through its contents whether it is a forgery, a literary fraud or the revealed word of an inspired Prophet ... If we accept it as a forgery, as the Christian scholars say, then the most surprising fact which baffles explanation is how a man of such remarkable and superb talent forged this Gospel has remained unknown to this day.[16]

1981

In conjunction with the London-based Union of Muslim Organisations in 1981 a handsome little volume for English-speaking Muslim children was published entitled *The Prophets*. The prefatory 'Letter to Muslim Parents and Children' states: 'This book has been written for your children so that they may know something about our great prophets'. Chapter 9 deals with Isa (Jesus). Under the section 'Isa (peace be on him) Is Taken Up', we read:

> Some of the Israelites did not believe in Isa (peace be on him). They were jealous. They reported lies to the Roman governor against him. At last Judas, one of those disciples who were with him, decided to betray him. Saint Barnabas, one of his closest friends, has written about this. Isa (peace be on him) was staying in a disciple's house. Judas had told the Roman soldiers that they should catch the man whom he would kiss on the cheek. He went and kissed Isa (peace be on him). But the whole room became dark and there was confusion. When the room became bright, the soldiers caught Judas because Allah had changed his features. He looked like Isa (peace be on him). He protested. He appealed. But the soldiers laughed. They put a crown of thorns on him and said,

thinking he was Isa (peace be on him), 'Now you are the King of the Jews.'

He was taken to the gallows and crucified.

Most of the disciples of Isa (peace be on him) were either confused or believed that it was Isa (peace be on him) who was crucified. Some of them went and buried him. Later on some of them dug up the grave and took away the dead body and told people that he had gone to Heaven.

But Allah had lifted him up at the time and the Roman soldiers had come.

Saint Barnabas, one of his nearest disciples, says in his written account, that he was not crucified and that he was alive. He came in the company of angels in order to tell his mother that he was alive so that she could get some peace of mind.[17]

All the world loves a mystery, and there is something about the idea of a 'suppressed, lost or secret' gospel which attracts instant attention. There are a host of so-called apocryphal gospels, acts, epistles and apocalypses with similarities to the several types of writing in the canonical New Testament. Early in the Church's history, the authorities were vexed as to which books outside the canon (the authoritative list of books accepted as Holy Scripture) might have merit, or had been rejected in accordance with rather arbitrary decisions.

The use of the term 'apocrypha' is unsatisfactory and confusing. It comes from the Greek meaning 'hidden' or 'secret', and soon acquired the connotation of 'spurious' or 'false'. Currently, the term is applied to a variety of biblical writings. Foremost amongst these is the Apocrypha, Jewish writings which Catholics, Anglicans and certain other Christian groups place between the Old and New Testaments. This includes such texts as Judith, Ecclesiasticus and the two Books of the Maccabees.

The so-called 'New Testament apocrypha' is a fascinating collection of works of which the New Testament scholar M.S. Enslin has said: 'Many of them are trivial, some are highly theatrical, some are disgusting; nonetheless, they may be properly styled religious.'[18] The collection includes Gospels of Peter, Thomas, and Philip; Acts of John, Paul, and Andrew; Epistles of Christ and Abgarus, and Lentulus; and Apocalypses of Peter, Thomas and Paul. The gamut of New Testament literature is presented. This apocryphal New Testament is in no way analogous to the Jewish writings referred to above, for the former was never regarded as acceptable by orthodox

Christians; it was produced by and for schismatic or heretical groups, especially the Gnostics. Many of the New Testament apocryphal books served as heretical substitutes for canonical writings.

St. John's Gospel contains two passages which present a spirit that would seem to elicit new scriptural material: 'There were indeed many other signs that Jesus performed in the presence of his disciples, which are not recorded in this book' (John 20.30); 'There is much else that Jesus did. If it were all to be recorded in detail, I suppose the whole world could not hold the books that would be written' (John 21.25). As the New Testament scholar Robert Grant has put it, 'Gnostics and others may have proceeded to test this hypothesis.'[19] Even though the Church fathers roundly rejected the apocryphal gospels, sayings they contained that were attributed to Jesus were often accepted and used by them. Apparently, as Grant says, they felt there might be 'a little gold' in the 'mud' of the apocryphal material.

The books of the apocryphal New Testament have received regular serious scholarly attention, but not so the extremely spurious grouping known as 'modern apocrypha'. Of this collection Enslin says, 'without exception (they) are worthless trash and the rankest forgeries'.[20] This assortment includes such books as *The Aquarian Gospel, The Twenty-Ninth Chapter of Acts, The Confessions of Pontius Pilate* and *The Gospel of Josephus*.[21] Many of these works regularly reappear in bookshops as 'new and startling revelations', and most of them attempt to present 'the lost years of Jesus', those from his infancy to the time of his ministry at around age thirty. St. Luke's is the only canonical Gospel which includes a mention of Jesus' boyhood days: his questioning of the teachers in the temple at Jerusalem when he was twelve (Luke 2.40–52). It is this period of 'lost years' where fancy has been most active at churning out new gospels. A nineteenth-century document, *The Unknown Life of Jesus Christ*, is perennially being resurrected – most recently in *The Jesus Mystery* by Janet Bock[22] and A. Faber-Kaiser's *Jesus Died in Kashmir*.[23] These books take a line that is encountered in a number of popular Muslim polemical works, especially those of the Ahmadis. In *The Unknown Life*, Jesus spent the 'lost years' wandering with a caravan of merchants, and studying at the feet of the great Buddhas and brahmins in India.

Edgar Goodspeed analysed *The Unknown Life* in his book *Strange New Gospels*,[24] noting the attention it received in 1895 and 1926. In 1887 a Russian war correspondent, Nicholas Notovitch,

15

visited India and then Tibet, where at the lamasery of Himis he said he learned of the *Life of Saint Issa, Best of the Sons of Men*.[25] The influential philologist and religious writer Friedrich Max Müller argued that Notovitch's document did not appear in any of the great collections of Tibetan literature, and inquiries he presented to monastery authorities had indicated that the writing was a fraud. Despite the critique of Max Müller and others, the work continues to have a modest popular hearing.[26]

The Crucifixion of Jesus, by an Eye-Witness,[27] probably the work of a nineteenth-century rationalist, has been used by Muslim polemicists looking for proof that Jesus did not die on the cross. This is the story of Jesus as an Essene monk: everything concerning his ministry is explained by his being a part of this Jewish ascetic sect. The angel of annunciation was an Essene, as was Christ's father, Joseph. It was the Essenes who carried Jesus away after the Crucifixion and revived him with a special potion, the 'myrrh and aloes' of the Gospel story. The Ahmadi Muslims have been especially attracted to the account, and use it to fortify their contention that Jesus completed his ministry in the company of the lost tribes of Israel in Kashmir.

Goodspeed thinks the author of *The Crucifixion of Jesus* was a rationalist writer repeating ideas advanced by scholars like Heinrich Paulus and Karl August Von Hase, who believed Jesus did not suffer death on the cross but was later resuscitated.[28]

Aside from the occasional popular appeal, none of the 'modern apocrypha' are taken seriously by scholars today. Two gospels noted in Muslim apologetics which have attracted continued scholarly attention are those of Peter and Judas. Tabari, the tenth-century historian of Baghdad, maintains the view that a number of early Christians believed that Judas assumed the likeness of Jesus and was crucified in his stead.[29] Fragments of the second-century Gospel of Judas give a favourable evaluation of the traitor. Judas' betrayal is treated as a meritorious action delivering man from the power of the demiurge, the Gnostic subordinate deity who created the material world. Judas' behaviour made him the 'perfect Gnostic'. According to Irenaeus, the Judas gospel was used by the Cainites, a Gnostic sect which regarded the God of the Old Testament as responsible for the evil in the world and exalted those who withstood him – men like Cain and Esau.

There was a reluctance on the part of some early Christians to believe that Jesus, the Son of God, could really die. The second-century Bishop of Antioch, Ignatius, said that some Christians

16

taught that Jesus 'suffered in semblance'. Jesus only 'seemed' (*dokein*) to die physically (the Docetic heresy): either the crucified body was a phantom form or someone else took his place. Another Bishop of Antioch, Serapion, was asked his opinion about a certain Gospel of Peter being used in his diocese. According to Robert Grant, he at first settled the issue rather hastily by giving his permission for the book to be read.[30] Following a more careful analysis of a copy he was able to obtain from some Docetists, he withdrew his approval. Theodoret, fifth bishop of Cyrrhus, wrote that the Nazarenes (or Nasoreans), Jewish Christians claiming descent from Jesus' first disciples, used the Gospel of Peter.

Until 1886, the existence of *Peter* was known only from a few references; then, in the winter of that year, a fragment of it was found at Akhmin in Upper Egypt in the grave of a Christian monk. Edgar Hennecke, an expert on New Testament apocrypha, feels it contains 'no articulated Gnostic theology but ... indicates that such a theology is already on the way'.[31] Two items point in that direction: the account it gives of the Crucifixion casts doubt on the reality of Christ's sufferings – when crucified 'he held his peace, as though having no pain' – and the only utterance coming from him on the cross was 'My power, my power, thou has forsaken me.'

An intriguing possibility, which will be a point of inquiry in this book, was touched upon by Leonard St. Alban Wells in his discussion of the Gospel of Peter: 'It contains the germ, but not the fruit of the later Docetic heresy as seen at the full in the Qur'an and in the Gospel of Barnabas.'[32] Unfortunately, Wells does not elucidate the point; but in more recent times two scholars have seen in *The Gospel of Barnabas* traces of early Jewish Christian apocryphal material.

Luigi Cirillo with Michel Frémaux produced in 1977 the first complete French translation of *Barnabas*.[33] Cirillo made a strenuous effort to trace its possible origins and backgrounds and indicated a layer of apocryphal material that was distinct from the obvious medieval layer of the gospel. He felt the former originated from one literary unit which was used by the medieval writer. The idea that 'Fra Marino' used some primitive text has been suggested by a number of observers, as we shall see.

The Hebrew University expert on early Christian history, Shlomo Pines, suggested the 'milieu of Jewish Christianity' for a primitive text of *Barnabas* (see page 11).[34] Jewish Christian history is complicated by the existence of considerable political pressures and a myriad of sectarian divisions. The tension between Christians and Jews relaxed somewhat when James, Jesus' brother, took over as the head of the Church in Jerusalem. James was anxious to have good relations with the Jewish leaders as his own convictions were strongly legalistic; and he was embarrassed by Paul's presence in Jerusalem because of the latter's strong contacts with Gentiles and concessions to their way of life. Until AD 62, when James was put to death by the Sanhedrin, the Jerusalem Christians zealously demonstrated their loyalty to Judaism. This was also when the Nazarenes were said to have been driven from Palestine after a quarrel with other Christians.

The Jewish revolt against Roman occupation in the years AD 66–70 made the position of the Church in Jerusalem increasingly difficult; and a generation later, during the reign of Hadrian, a second revolt (AD 132–135) was attempted. On the emperor's orders, the city of Jerusalem was levelled and a pagan city called Aelia Capitolina built on the site. Circumcised Jews were barred from entrance to the new city. Apparently, just before the Roman siege began, Christians decided to flee to a place of safety; and the fourth-century Church historian Eusebius of Caesarea writes that they went to the Gentile city of Pella, east of the Jordan. There Jewish Christians, fastidious about maintaining separateness from Gentiles, remained scattered and isolated from the general life of the Church and drifted into a variety of curious practices and heresies. Writers in the second and fourth centuries tell of various groups who are probably survivors of that exiled Jewish Christianity.

It has been suggested that the Ebionites ('poor' in Hebrew), who were mentioned earlier, were directly related to the Jerusalem community which also called itself 'the poor'. Epiphanius, the fourth-century Bishop of Salamis, described and attacked in his *Panarion* every heresy known to him from the beginning of the Church. His catalogue includes the Nazarenes, whom he says continued to obey much of the Jewish law and used a version of the Gospel in Aramaic known as the 'Gospel according to the Hebrews'.[35]

Under the influence of unorthodox Jewish sects in the Jordan region, Jewish Christian groups engaged in the wildest kind of elaboration of the faith. Early in the second century a prophet named Elkesai appeared. His followers, the Elkesaites, possessed a sacred writing which contained the revelation given to their founder in which Jesus appeared as a mountain ninety-six miles high! The Elkesaites held beliefs similar to those of the Ebionites

18

and rejected sacrifices and certain biblical books, especially the epistles of Paul. They also maintained a Docetic view of the person of Christ; but, as one commentator put it, like the rivers of Damascus, they, along with other curious sects, flowed out to the edge of the desert and vanished.

The Bishop of Bradford, A. W. F. Blunt, in his 1923 commentary on *The Acts of the Apostles*[36] gives a view, with no quoted sources, which is to me intriguing and one we explore in another context: 'The Elkesaites ... never had any life except, in the country east of the Dead Sea, but in the sixth century Mohammed lived for some time in an Elkesaite community, and to this fact may be due the strange mixture of Jewish and Christian elements which can be seen in the Koran.'[37] This extraordinary comment, like that given by Leonard St. Alban Wells concerning the Gospels of Peter and Barnabas, caused me to do a double-take when I first saw it. In themselves such remarks provide no more than intimations, but they suggest a worthwhile exploration which I will make later.

Shlomo Pines's attention was drawn to *The Gospel of Barnabas* by a colleague at the Hebrew University, David Flusser, who is also an expert on the history of the early Church. Flusser was struck by the observations on *Barnabas* of the Irish deistical writer John Toland in his 1718 treatise on the Ebionites, *Nazarenus*. Pines feels that 'Toland rightly pointed out this Gospel contains "Ebionite" elements'.[38] Among others he mentions the opposition to Paul (the Ebionites rejected him as an apostle), the issues of circumcision and unclean meat. As noted earlier (page 11), Pines indicates that the Muslim writer Biruni postulated a connection between the 'Ebionite Gospel' and the Gospel of *B. lam. s.*: 'In view of the peculiarities of the Arabic script, the possibility of the transformation of an Arabic form of the name of Barnabas into *B. lam. s.* can be envisaged.'[38]

Jan Slomp has, however, argued: 'As long as Professor Pines does not support his suggestion by stronger proofs it is possible to raise serious objections against his hypothesis.' Slomp thinks that if an early form of Barnabas' gospel was known to the companions of Muhammad, 'it is hard to understand why no Muslim tradition ever mentions it'.[39]

Despite this, the fact of a Jewish scholar of Pines's stature bringing scholarly attention to *Barnabas* and linking it to Jewish Christian sources has not gone unnoticed in Muslim polemical writings. Pines's interest began when the Oxford Islamic scholar Samuel Stern[40] mentioned a rambling 600-page manuscript, Abd

19

al-Jabbar's book on the proofs of Muhammad's prophecy, in the archives of Istanbul. Abd al-Jabbar was a tenth-century Muslim theologian and Chief Kadi of Rayy, a city which formerly stood on the site of modern Tehran. Pines noted that about 140 pages of the manuscript consisted of a much older Syriac account of what he considered to be Nazarene beliefs. Previously, the Jewish Christian Nazarenes had been known of only through the Church fathers' polemics against them. Jabbar's account created a flurry of academic excitement in 1966, and Flusser claimed the find to be 'as important for the story of the first Christians as the Dead Sea Scrolls were for understanding the pre-Christian background'.[41]

Pines's release of the material to the press and *Time* magazine added fuel to Muslim polemics concerning early Christianity. Mumtaz Ahmad Faruqui writes: 'It has been shown that quite a number of the early and true Jewish followers of Jesus, in the early decades after his death, regarded him as another prophet of Israel, and denounced ... Paul for preaching his message to the Gentiles.'[42] Much of the Syriac account copied by Jabbar consisted of polemics against Paul – an argument Jabbar continued in lengthy detail – and remind us of some of the polemical material from Pakistan already quoted. Whereas Jesus and his disciples had observed the law of Moses, Christians had subsequently changed the laws and adopted the customs and institutions of the pagan Romans. A formula used three times by Jabbar was that it was not the Romans who became Christians but the Christians who became Romanised. Though the corruption began soon after Jesus' ministry, the chief culprits were Paul and, later, Constantine.[43]

According to Jabbar, it was difficult even for a trained theologian to get a correct statement out of Christians about their beliefs because of the various sectarian differences. One portion of the Istanbul manuscript receiving little attention from either Muslim polemicists or the press was an apocryphal account of the Passion which for Jabbar served as proof that the Koran was right and the crucified man was not Jesus. Unfortunately Jabbar does not tell us the source of the account, but it is clear he thought it came from the canonical New Testament. It is remarkably similar to early Muslim commentaries on the koranic text, and also evocative of the story of the Passion as presented in *Barnabas*.

Jabbar's unknown gospel states that Judas apparently tricked the Jews by delivering to them another man in the place of Jesus (in *Barnabas*, it is Judas himself who was Jesus' substitute on the cross). This unknown victim denied explicitly before Herod and

Pilate that he was the Messiah, as Judas does in *Barnabas*. Herod, not Pilate, took a basin of water and washed his hands of the accused man's blood to show he found no guilt in him. Herod then imprisoned the supposed Jesus for the night, but the next morning he was seized by angry Jews who tortured and finally crucified him.

It is, however, Pines's report of Jabbar's attacks on Paul which attracted the attention of Muslim writers. Paul's 'subversion of the original pure Jewish Christian faith' is their interest. As Mumtaz Ahmad Faruqui continues his argument: 'Paul set up a creed of which Jesus knew nothing. He not only ignored the historical Jesus for the mythical Christ, but he also maintained his apostolic independence of those who lived with and saw Jesus, and he held himself aloof from the teachings of Jesus as contained in the gospels.'[44] In those words Faruqui sounds very much like the author of *The Gospel of Barnabas*. That book's last chapter ends, as it began, with a snipe at the apostle:

> After Jesus had departed, the disciples scattered through the different parts of Israel and of the world, and the truth, hated of Satan, was persecuted, as it always is, by falsehood. For certain evil men, pretending to be disciples, ... preached, and yet preach, that Jesus is the Son of God, among whom Paul is deceived.[45]

CHAPTER TWO

'The Gospel in Its Present Form'

'Ata ur-Rahim in *Jesus, A Prophet of Islam*[46] presents the apostle Barnabas as the leader of those Christians who opposed Paul's 'new gospel', a perversion of the simple monotheism preached by Jesus to the disciples. On a purely surface level, the picture of Barnabas and Paul in opposition over the direction of early Christianity has a certain appeal – particularly in the light of the views of Jewish Christian sects like the Ebionites. This has been a feature of popular polemics of a number of 'liberal' Christian and Muslim writers.

The biblical record of Barnabas is fairly clear, with a few indications that there was some disagreement between him and Paul but nothing like what has been suggested by writers like 'Ata ur-Rahim. The Barnabas of the New Testament, as one-time Cambridge professor of divinity F. C. Burkitt has written, 'is an interesting personality of whom we would gladly know more, not only before he comes upon the scene in *Acts* and after he has left it, but also to his opinions and development during the time we do hear something of him'. [47] Barnabas was a Jewish Levite of Cyprus and became one of the earliest Christian disciples at Jerusalem. He seems to have been the leader of the Church in Antioch, where the term 'Christian' was first applied to the followers of Jesus. It was Barnabas who introduced Paul to the other apostles, which opened the door for him into the Jerusalem Christian community. Barnabas' support of Paul had a determining influence on the other Christian leaders. In the fifteenth chapter of the Acts of the Apostles, Barnabas defended the claims of the Gentile Christians at the Church council in Jerusalem. This meant an enormous amount

of support for Paul. The pre-eminence St. Luke gives of 'Barnabas and Paul' indicates Barnabas' early importance over the one who would soon completely overshadow him. In the city of Lystra in Asia Minor the two missionaries were greeted with enthusiasm, Barnabas being honoured by the natives with the title of 'Zeus' while Paul was simply named 'Hermes', the spokesman.

The notion of theological antagonism between the two is based on the separation of Barnabas from Paul at Antioch after the Jerusalem conference. This occurred over the matter of Barnabas taking his young cousin, John Mark, on a new missionary journey. Earlier, Mark had left Paul and his company in Cyprus and returned to Jerusalem; this 'defection' was for Paul sufficient grounds for dropping him from the next effort. Barnabas was devoted to his cousin, and despite Paul's objection took Mark with him to Cyprus. We read in Acts: 'And there arose a sharp contention, so that they separated from each other.' The rift is further described in Paul's Letter to the Galatians with the discussion of the 'Judaizing' party of Christians who were against eating at table with Gentiles. Paul was displeased with his old friend's seeming siding with the 'Judaizers' and said, 'even Barnabas was carried away and played false like the rest'.

Barnabas' theological position in the early Church was something of a middle course between those who favoured Paul's 'open' requirements for a mission to the Gentiles and the 'Judaizers' who were still wishing to maintain restrictions of the Mosaic law. Like Peter, Barnabas had great sympathy with the community at Jerusalem, but he was hardly the advocate of a 'pure Jewish Christianity' some writers have projected. He is the traditional founder of the Cypriot Church, and legend asserts that when his relics were discovered in fifth-century Cyprus a copy of the Gospel of St. Matthew written in his own hand was found lying on his breast. Writers like 'Ata ur-Rahim have insisted that was 'the original Gospel of Barnabas'.[48]

No group of Muslims has made greater polemical use of the Gospel of Barnabas than the Ahmadiyya movement, founded in Pakistan in the latter part of the nineteenth century by Hazrat Mirza Ghulam Ahmad when he announced that Allah had appointed him the Messiah. (The lesser known Muslim fundamentalists Jamá et e Islamic – the Muslim Brethren – have also shown great interest in the gospel.) Orthodox Muslims have always accepted the Greek title Christ ('Messiah') for Jesus, and it is used eleven times in the Koran with no particular explanation being given for its interpretation. For this deviation and others, the Ahmadis are viewed as heretical by other Muslims; yet they carry out extensive evangelism in northern Africa, often side by side with other Muslim missionaries. More than any other Muslim group they have developed the koranic denial of Jesus' death into an elaborate scenario. Ghulam Ahmad had found a tomb in Srinagar said to be that of the Kashmiri prophet Yus Asaph, and received a revelation that it was the tomb of Jesus who had died in Kashmir at the age of 120. A. Faber-Kaiser explains that having left Palestine, 'Jesus seems to have travelled under the alias of "Yus Asaph"' and claims, with the Ahmadis, that the name is the Arabic form of 'Jesus the Gatherer'[49] (the name for Jesus in the Koran is Isa). In 1890 the Ahmadi founder 'under Divine inspiration' declared that Jesus did not die on the cross but, having survived death, travelled to Afghanistan and subsequently to Kashmir in search of the ten tribes of Israel who had migrated there after their deliverance from bondage under Nebuchadnezzar.

The Ahmadi scenario for Jesus' survival of the Crucifixion is highly inventive and, as we shall see, suggestive of some details found in both Gnostic writings and early Muslim commentaries on the koranic denial. Pontius Pilate was certain of the innocence of Jesus and therefore, goaded by his dream-troubled wife, devised a plot to save his prisoner's life. As a responsible officer of the Roman empire he could not openly come to the forefront, but he was nevertheless the master-mind behind the whole scheme and the chief actor in the drama; also privy to the scheme were Joseph of Arimathea and Nicodemus. Conveniently, Pilate chose Friday afternoon as the time for Jesus' Crucifixion so that he would not be able to remain on the cross after sunset – the following day being the Sabbath. Joseph and Nicodemus brought Jesus to consciousness, as in *The Crucifixion of Jesus by an Eye-Witness*, by using a so-called 'special ointment'. Jesus recovered, making his way from Palestine through Persia to Afghanistan and finally to Kashmir; even the route he took is charted in Ahmadi material.[50]

A book which developed this argument exhaustively was the 416-page work by the Ahmadi Muslim Al-Haj Khwaja Nazir Ahmad, *Jesus in Heaven on Earth* (a name given by Ahmadis and others to Kashmir).[51] It first appeared in 1952 and was widely read in Pakistan and India as well as the Near East. Nazir Ahmad was once the senior advocate of Pakistan's Supreme Court and took an eager interest in *The Gospel of Barnabas*, concerning which book he presents a strange logic: 'Unless the original copy which was rejected by the Gelasian Council is produced, or in the absence of proof that the present copy is different from the copy which was recovered from the tomb of St. Barnabas, the Gospel in its present form must be accepted.'[52]

Along with the altered tradition of Barnabas' relics, including 'the original gospel of Barnabas', the mentioning of 'a gospel of Barnabas' in two ancient listings of apocryphal works has been sufficient proof of Barnabas' authenticity for Muslim writers utilising the document. Both the so-called Gelasian Decree 'Of Books' (not later than the sixth century) and the seventh-century Greek 'List of Sixty Books' give the name of 'a Gospel under the name of Barnabas', but the name is all we have. There is no Gospel of Barnabas 'written in his own hand', no fragments of a 'lost gospel' of Barnabas, no quotations from a Gospel of Barnabas in the Church fathers; the 'Gospel in its present form' (to use Nazir Ahmad's words) is in Vienna, and the history of that Italian manuscript is in itself a fascinating story.

Despite latter-day attempts to link *The Gospel of Barnabas* with the apostle Barnabas and the disputations of early Jewish Christianity, the extant gospel was basically unknown in the Muslim world until 1734, when George Sale translated the Koran into English. As Temple Gairdner[53] wrote, Sale gave 'a chance mention of it' in the introduction and commentary to that translation. In his copious and still useful notes, Sale refers to a gospel 'which gives ... part of the history of Jesus with circumstances too curious to be omitted'. George Sale's translation of the Koran was the first full translation into any modern language except for what is termed the 'lamentable French version' of André Du Ryer in 1649 (which was rendered into English the same year by Alexander Ross). Sale's Koran is still published, and used in koranic studies. As Sir Edward Denison Ross claims in the introduction: 'the present work presents to the Western student all the essentials of preliminary study of Islam' – and that, to a certain extent, is still true.[54]

Until fairly recently, Sale was the sole source of the existence of a Spanish manuscript of *Barnabas* and the Fra Marino account of the finding of the gospel in Pope Sixtus V's library. The Spanish version was seen by Sale when it was in the possession of the rector of Hedley in Hampshire, a Dr Holme. It later passed into the hands of Thomas Monkhouse, a Fellow of Queen's College, Oxford, and was said 'to have disappeared from sight'. The Revd Joseph White saw the Spanish version while it was still in the possession of Monkhouse, and in his Bampton Lectures (Oxford, 1784) he gave

25

translation of the chapters dealing with the crucifixion of Judas. A later comparison of these sections with the Italian, as recorded by the Raggs, revealed very little difference. Dr White's reference was the last known one to the Spanish text; and then, surprisingly, in 1976 a partial copy of that text seen by Sale and reproduced in part by White was reported to exist in the University of Sydney's Fisher Library as part of the great collection of Sir Charles Nicholson, its first chancellor.

The inside front cover has the armorial book-plate of Nicholson and a note: 'Transcribed from ms. in possession of the Revd Mr. Edm. Callamy who bought it at the Decease of Mr. George Sale ... and now gave me at the Decease of Mr. John Nickolls, 1745'.[55] It would seem that the manuscript, like a number of other items in the Fisher Library, was purchased in Dublin, where two of Callamy's descendants resided. The importance of the Sydney manuscript will be discussed in Chapter 4.

According to the preface to his translation, George Sale heard about *The Gospel of Barnabas* through Bernard de la Monnoye, who mentioned it in *Mengiana* (1715)[56] and the aforementioned John Toland, who noted in *Nazarenus* (1718) that gospel's affinity of 'making of Jesus a mere man' with 'the ancient Ebionite or Nazarene system'. *Nazarenus* called attention to the position of the Ebionites in the development of the early Church. Toland, a remarkable freethinker, was brought up, near Londonderry in Ireland, as a Catholic but later became a Protestant. In 1696 he published *Christianity Not Mysterious*, in which he sought to show that all the doctrine of scripture as Christian revelation could be interpreted rationally. The Irish Parliament condemned his book; and his later writings in England included an attempt to explain the miracles in the Old Testament.

Toland's discussion of *Barnabas* helps us unravel its whereabouts in the eighteenth century:

It is a Mahometan [Muslim] Gospel never publicly made known among Christians tho they have much talked about the Mahometans acknowledging the Gospel ... The learned gentleman who has been so kind as to communicate it to me [viz. Mr. Cramer, Counsellor to the King of Prussia, but residing in Amsterdam] had it out of the library of a person of great name and authority in the said city; who during his life was often heard to put a high value on the piece.[57]

26

Elsewhere, Toland gives the impression that his discovery was unique: 'There's but one copy of it in Christendom, accidentally discovered by me in Amsterdam', the year of discovery being 1709.[58] Jan Slomp thinks it likely the 'person of great name and authority' was the Italian scholar Gregorio Leti, father-in-law of Thomas Mongey who in 1718 wrote about *Barnabas* in *Bibliothèque Angloise on Histoire Littéraire de la Gran Bretagne*. Leti was the official historian of the city of Amsterdam, and his library was sold in 1701, so Slomp's idea fits the known circumstances of the gospel being in Amsterdam.[59] The link with the Italian Leti also takes us back to the manuscript's country of origin.

Gregorio Leti is an intriguing person. He is just the type to become involved with a work like *Barnabas*, and if he had lived a century and a half earlier, he would seem a likely candidate for authorship. Leti was born in Milan of a Bolognese family in 1630 and studied with the Jesuits at Cosenza and Rome. His uncle, the Bishop of Aquapendente, was shocked at his nephew's ideas on religion and afraid he would be contaminated by these heretical views. Leti set off on many wanderings in central Europe. He became a Calvinist in Geneva, and lived successfully there and in London and Amsterdam. He was the author of many books on a variety of topics, including biographies of Elizabeth I and Pope Sixtus V; the latter volume, though popular, was vigorously condemned by the Church. Leti holds some kind of record as earning seventeen condemnations in thirty-five years in the Index of Prohibited Books.[60]

The German diplomat J. F. Cramer next comes to own the gospel – perhaps he bought it from Leti's large library – and he presented it to one of the period's great collectors of books, Prince Eugene of Savoy. Along with the prince's extensive library, the Italian manuscript of *The Gospel of Barnabas* found its way into the imperial library of Vienna.

George Sale's 1734 mention of *The Gospel of Barnabas* initiated a certain Muslim fascination with the manuscript, but it was not until 1907, when two English scholars translated the Italian manuscript, that a strong Muslim polemic employing *Barnabas* developed. Lonsdale Ragg and his wife Laura became interested in the quarto of 255 leaves in the imperial library shortly before the former was appointed chaplain to the Anglican communities in Bologna and Venice. Ragg is in the best tradition of Church of England clergymen of the period whose intellectual interests were many-sided. He wrote two books on Dante (an interest which helped with

27

his research into *Barnabas*), painted 'tree-portraits' and was editor of *Tree Lover* in 1932. His clerical career covered a long period: he served as Vice-Principal of Cuddesdon College and Vice-Chancellor at Lincoln Cathedral, and held several European posts, including that of Archdeacon of Gibraltar, which he held until his death in 1945. One of his obituary notices speaks of his 'spare figure, intellectual head and genial smile'. His wife was a faithful collaborator in many of his pursuits.[61]

In the preface to their book on *Barnabas*, the Raggs state: 'The translators encountered many unforeseen difficulties during the four years in which the work has been in their hands; much of the translation has been hewn out on pilgrimage, or in small hotel rooms, and far from books of reference.'[62] That makes their achievement even more remarkable, for their critical analysis remains the definitive work on the subject. It is their translation which has been the basis of all subsequent reproductions of the Vienna document.

The Raggs present a general opinion that the Italian manuscript was probably 'a deliberate forgery of the latter half of the sixteenth century'. That date could be established on evidence of the paper used itself. It is described as 'a somewhat coarse and stout "cotton-paper" ... with a water-mark no oriental paper ever bore'. An expert the Raggs consulted noted the anchor within a circle as being distinctly Italian, and the particular form it took on these leaves clearly belonged to the second half of the sixteenth century.

The handwriting tries to present an archaic flavour to the document, and suggests a style a century earlier. Italian scholars who analysed the writing noted an intermingling of Tuscan and North Italian characteristics and were inclined to believe it to be a Tuscan original copied by a Venetian scribe or perhaps the other way round. The many Arabic marginal notes throughout the text were also of interest and were filled with mistakes, giving the appearance of a European attempting to translate Italian phrases into an imperfect Arabic. The purpose of the marginal glosses is 'somewhat mysterious' to the translators, and in an article before the publication of the book, Lonsdale Ragg quotes F. C. Burkitt's remark that 'their function may have been to protect the MS from destruction at the hands of Moslems ignorant of western languages'.[63]

A decisive point in placing the manuscript in the Middle Ages is a tell-tale error the writer made concerning the Jewish Year of Jubilee, which was celebrated every fifty years in biblical times. It was a year when Jewish slaves regained their freedom and land reverted to its former owners (Leviticus 25). *Barnabas* makes the celebration a centenary event, and the mistake seemed to reveal an interesting possibility. Pope Boniface VIII proclaimed the first jubilee year for Roman Catholics in 1300, which brought thousands of pilgrims to Rome. Owing to that financial success, Clement VI altered Boniface's intention of having the celebration every hundred years, and shortened the period: the next jubilee was celebrated in 1350. This indicated to the Raggs the writer must have lived after 1300 but before 1350, which would have made him a contemporary of Dante Alighieri. That conveniently meshed with a Dantesque colouration in the gospel. The Raggs conclude: '[This] internal evidence ... would point, then, to an Italian original of AD 1300–50: unless, indeed, the "Jubilee" passage is capable of another explanation.'[64] Yet much else about the manuscript points to its having been written at least a century or two later.

The 'Jubilee' passage in Chapter 82 of *Barnabas* reads: 'And then through all the world will God be worshipped, and mercy received, insomuch that the year of jubilee, which now cometh every hundred years, shall by the Messiah be reduced to every year in every place.' In 1978, Jan Slomp offered another explanation. He stressed the word 'reduced' in the passage because the reduction to 1350 did not stop there. In 1470, the year of the jubilee became every twenty-five years. When Sixtus V (the pope of the Fra Marino story) ascended the throne in 1585, he started his reign with a jubilee, thus giving the impression that the holy father could name every or any year to be one of jubilee (1983–84 was declared an extraordinary jubilee by John Paul II). This tempts Slomp to suggest 1585 as the exact date for the 'Jubilee' passage.[65]

Though about a third of the material in *Barnabas* has been derived from other sources the four canonical Gospels were shown by the Raggs to form the fundamental substratum of the manuscript. Curiously, there are no direct quotations from the Koran, and the writer is far more conversant with Christian than with Muslim scriptures. There is, however, a large amount of distinctly Muslim material, often in the form of long discourses put into the mouth of Jesus. The magical transformation of Judas and his arrest, trial and Crucifixion in place of Jesus are for the translators 'developments of hints in the Koran'. The Raggs felt that '*Barnabas* performs the part of a commentator – unless indeed he has been working up a separate document now lost to us'.[66] This suggestion has been entertained by others, as we have seen.

Barnabas is at variance with the Koran on a number of important and minor points. First, it states that Mary experienced the birth of Jesus without pain, which contradicts the Koran. The Raggs think this passage may constitute 'a trace of an apocryphal gospel', but indicate that the birth without pain was also 'an accepted tradition of Latin medieval Christianity'. A variety of Gnostic-style parables, miracles and stories are included in the gospel, yet certain well-known accounts which have clear Gnostic literary parallels, such as those of Jesus speaking from the cradle, the appearance of a miraculous spring for mother and child in the desert and the infant Jesus' creation of birds from clay, are not to be found there.

Not only does Jesus foretell the coming of Muhammad in *Barnabas*, but the Prophet *is* the promised Messiah. It does not occur to the writer that the appellation 'Christ' is the Greek word for 'Messiah', and he seems equally unaware that in the Koran Jesus is 'al Masih' (Messiah). (The Arabic and first Urdu translations of *Barnabas* tried to hide the contradiction by writing *Masiya* instead of *al Masih*!) The Gospel role of John the Baptist as Jesus' forerunner is eliminated in *Barnabas*, and that position is given to Jesus. Neither John nor his father, Zachariah, who are both mentioned several times in the Koran, ever appears in *Barnabas*.

The gospel makes Muhammad to be the Messiah in no uncertain terms, and the Raggs ask if he also is accorded the title of Paraclete, as Sale had suggested. 'Paraclete' is the Gospel of John's epithet for the Holy Spirit and has been traditionally translated 'comforter'. The Latin Vulgate translation is 'advocate', which is preferred by many modern commentators. Scholars have noted the affinity of a koranic reference to the Paraclete of St. John's Gospel, which has: 'But when your Advocate has come, whom I will send you from the Father ... he will bear witness to me' (John 15.26). Sura 61.6 of the Koran presents Jesus as saying to the 'Israelites': 'I am sent forth to you by Allah to confirm the Torah already revealed and to give news of an apostle that will come after me whose name is Ahmad.' That last word has usually been interpreted as being another name for Muhammad.

In *Barnabas*, the proclamation that Jesus is 'giving news of an apostle' who will follow him is not veiled. The name Muhammad is repeatedly used, but whether a precise identification between the Christian Paraclete and Muhammad is presented in *Barnabas*, the Raggs say, 'No more ... and no less than does the Qoran itself'.[67]

Further evidence for accepting the gospel as a medieval creation is the sometimes incredible ignorance it shows of first-century

Palestine: no gospel writer of the first centuries would make those mistakes. Arch-enemies Herod, Pilate and the Jewish high priest Caiaphas are frequently found hobnobbing together. Caiaphas begs Pilate to procure a decree from the Roman senate making it a capital offence to call Jesus 'God' or 'Son of God' – and this decree is posted up in the temple, engraved on copper! There are a number of geographical errors: the writer is apparently of the opinion that one can sail by boat to Nazareth.

The Raggs note a considerable medieval colouring to the gospel. The picturesque description of the summer season in Palestine is far more suggestive of *la bella Italia* than of first-century Palestine: there are references to stone quarries, ships, sailors, wine casks and feudal-sounding land division which are redolent of someone living in medieval Italy. Jesus' friends Mary, Martha and Lazarus are presented as proprietors of whole villages as if they had been feudal lords and ladies.

These touches are especially interesting to Lonsdale Ragg as an expert on Dante. He considers the description of the pains and cries of the damned in the gospel 'strongly reminiscent' of the Italian poet; the picture of hell in *Barnabas* is remarkably similar to that in the master's *Inferno*. Despite this, the translators make the observation that 'occasional inaccuracies are outweighed by a very general and intelligent knowledge alike of the Old Testament and the New'.[68] Undoubtedly the writer was well versed in the Latin Vulgate and, like the Koran, his gospel 'contains much beautiful teaching on the subject of prayer'.

The final point in the introductory notes returns to the question of a Gnostic *Gospel of Barnabas* behind the Italian manuscript. The Raggs say: 'Assuming, ... for the sake of an argument, that an original Gnostic *Barnabas* or a Latin version of the same, fell into the hands of a Christian renegade of the fourteenth or fifteenth century – it would give him at once a title for his great missionary pamphlet, and a vast amount of material to work on'.[69] The translators take note, as have Muslim polemicists, of the 'prefatory and valedictory denunciations of St. Paul' in the gospel.[70] These accusations give *Barnabas* the air of an apology by a convert seeking to justify his claims.

It is an irony that the 1907 publication of the Vienna manuscript had the effect of a death-blow to scholarly regard in the West; and yet in the Muslim world it initiated a strong polemical interest which has continued down to the present. For Western scholars the matter was settled: *Barnabas* was a forgery, devoid of any value.

31

The Raggs' critical introduction was practically ignored by Muslim writers, but their English translation became the basis of a 1908 Arabic translation which was reprinted many times. This in turn was the basis for further translations into Urdu, Persian, and Indonesian. Until the Raggs' book appeared, the text of *The Gospel of Barnabas* was not available to the wider public. With its translation into Arabic and other Muslim languages, Christians in Islamic countries, unlike those in the West, could not afford to ignore the existence of the strange book. Unknown to the Clarendon Press, the Raggs' English translation was published in Pakistan several times by a number of houses, most recently in 1981. Unlike previous editions, this publication contains the critical introduction but also a foreword which disclaims the importance of any critical analysis of the gospel (see pages 12–13).[71] Eight years earlier, another pirated English edition appeared in Karachi through the auspices of the Pakistani chapter of the World Muslim Congress and was promoted by articles in *The Pakistan Times*. It sold more than 12,000 copies in a few months.

As previously noted, Muslim interest in *Barnabas* has ranged from its being used by a sheikh of Cairo's prestigious al-Azhar in his religious instruction to its appearance in polemical works aimed at Western Christian readers. The seriousness with which the gospel is taken by some is vividly expressed in a small volume entitled *The Prophets* (see pages 13–14), whose author's expressed intention is to introduce young Muslims to the great prophets of Islam.[72] *Barnabas* is the avowed source for its presentation of Isa's (Jesus') last days. This incredible acceptance of a volume whose historical value has been termed 'exactly nil' by Western Christian scholars speaks loudly and points to a major division of understanding of the basis and formation of Christian scriptural tradition. *The Prophets* is no polemical tract initiated by an exotic Muslim sect; it carries the imprimatur of the Union of Muslim Organisations of the United Kingdom.

The Egyptian scholar G. C. Anawati writes: 'The appearance of a forgery entitled the Gospel of Barnabas put into the hands of the Muslim polemicists ... a new weapon whose effects on the ordinary public, and even on some insufficiently informed members of universities are felt even today.'[73] A decade has passed, and those words still have poignancy.

CHAPTER THREE

The Gospel Harmonised: The Contents of *The Gospel of Barnabas*

The word *Injil* (Gospel) is always used for the Christian revelation in the Koran: it entered Arabic from either Syriac or Ethiopic and occurs twelve times in the Muslim holy book. *Injil* is associated particularly with Jesus, as in Sura 5.46: 'We [Allah] sent forth Jesus, the son of Mary, confirming the Torah already revealed, and gave him the *Gospel*, in which there is guidance and light.'

It is difficult to know whether the word is used here to refer to the gospel Jesus preached during his lifetime or to the Christian scriptures, though it has been suggested by a number of Muslim commentators that *Injil* was different from the canonical Gospels held by Christians. In the eyes of some Islamic writers, the scriptures of both Jews and Christians have been corrupted. This 'corruption' (*tahrif*) was, according to the tenth-century commentator Biruni, an alteration of the biblical text. Others, including Tabari, writing at the same period, and the great fourteenth-century Arab historian Khaldun, saw the Christian scriptures as an incorrect interpretation.[74] The modern commentator Yusuf 'Ali goes further and states that 'the *Injil* spoken of by the Qur'an is not the New Testament. It is not the four Gospels now received as canonical. It is the single Gospel which, Islam teaches, was revealed to Jesus, and which he taught. Fragments of it survive in the received canonical Gospels and in some others of which traces survive'.[75] Yusuf 'Ali cites in the latter category the apocryphal infancy gospels and *The Gospel of Barnabas*. Several touches in the

Koran have clear parallels in at least two of those infancy gospels which have survived: Jesus speaking from the cradle (5.110ff. and 19.29ff.); creating birds from clay (3.49 and 5.110ff.); and a miraculous spring appearing for the mother and child (19.22ff.). The first and last accounts can be found in the Arabic Infancy Gospel. The Infancy Gospel of Thomas has a detailed story of a five-year-old Jesus creating twelve sparrows from clay while playing with his friends.

In his foreword to the 1981 Al-Kitab edition of *The Gospel of Barnabas*, Qazi Muhammad Hafizullah cites the absence of these accounts from the gospel as proof that 'No Muslim, or renegade to Islam from Christianity of Judaism was, therefore, the author of the Gospel'.[76] In his view, if the author 'had read the Quran [he] could not have failed to mention the above miracles also'. We shall return to a discussion of these accounts in Chapter 5.

The Australian Islamic scholar John Bowman has made the suggestion that the Muslim claim of there being one original Gospel may originate from the use of a gospel harmony, the Syrian Diatessaron, by Muhammad and others in early Islam.[77] The problem of having four separate Gospels containing minor contradictions and differences was a difficulty in the early Church and was solved by some Christians in one of two ways: the Ebionites used a version of Matthew exclusively, and the second-century heretic Marcion accepted Luke as the only true Gospel. Another approach was to harmonise the differences among the four Gospels. Gospel harmonies used to be popular in New Testament studies: I possess a well-worn example used by my grandfather and father at Southern Lutheran Seminary. It consists of four columned pages showing the similarities among the four Gospels and minimising the differences.

The second-century Syrian Gnostic Tatian was the first to compile a continuous narrative of the four Gospels which was known as the Diatessaron (formed from the Greek for 'through' plus 'four'). The work was circulated widely in the Syriac-speaking Churches and was their standard text of the Gospels until the fifth century, when it was gradually replaced by the four separate Gospels as in the rest of the Church. It is said that Rabbula, fifth-century Bishop of Edessa, replaced the Diatessaron with the Peshitta text of the New Testament (the official Syriac translation) because Tatian was a heretic. The only complete text of the Diatessaron to remain is the Arabic one translated from a Syriac manuscript in the ninth century.

Bowman stated his belief that Muhammad was influenced by the Diatessaron. He said that for several years he

> sought an answer to the problem of why it is that the Old Testament personages in the Qur'an are of the patriarchal period with few exceptions; allied with them as if of the same generation are Zacharias, Mary, Jesus and John. I believe the answer is that Muhammad gained his knowledge of the Old Testament from the Diatessaron, the Harmonised Gospel.[78]

Bowman gives impressive evidence in showing how, with few exceptions, the Old Testament figures of the Diatessaron are the same as those of the Koran; even the spelling of their names is identical in many cases. Bowman is convinced of the important debt Islam owes to Syrian Christianity and certain that, as we shall see in Chapter 5, the 'imperfect and garbled forms of Christianity' (as described by William Muir in 1878) which Muhammad knew were those of the Syrian heresies of the Nestorians and the Monophysites condemned by the fifth-century Church Councils of Ephesus and Chalcedon. Nestorians believed that there were two separate persons in the Incarnate Christ, the one divine and the other human, as opposed to the orthodox doctrine that Christ was a single person, at once God and man. Monophysitism (from the Greek for 'one' and 'nature') said that in the person of the Incarnate Christ there was but a single nature and that divine. The Egyptian and Ethiopian Christians follow this view, and both heresies were active in missionary work in Arabia, continuing to use the Diatessaron long after it had been replaced in orthodox Syrian Christianity.

Jan Slomp considers *Barnabas* to be a conscious attempt at imitating a Diatessaron. Canon and Mrs Ragg had noted that 'though about one-third of the bulk' of the gospel 'is derived from other sources, yet the four canonical Gospels may be shown to form the fundamental substratum of the whole document ... though a very unscientific harmony of the Gospels is implied'.[79] As Slomp indicates, the reader of *Barnabas* is struck by its sheer length.[80] The 222 chapters remind one of a gospel harmony, and one which employs other New Testament books as well: of the twenty-seven books in the New Testament, references are made directly or indirectly to at least nineteen. Despite the acid attacks on Paul in the gospel, there are, according to the Raggs, traces of a majority of his epistles. This is another of the many incongruities of the document.

More importantly, the author of *Barnabas* uses the Gospels as the

35

framework of his narrative. Like those of Matthew and Luke, his book begins with the annunciation, nativity and circumcision; it has Matthew's visit of the Magi and massacre of the innocents as well as Luke's finding of the boy Jesus in the temple. Like the New Testament Gospels, the central portion of *Barnabas* deals with Jesus' ministry and the last portion records the Passion and Crucifixion – albeit including the bizarre substitution of Judas for Jesus.

Slomp presents an admirable case for *Barnabas* being a type of Diatessaron. He studied a thirteenth- or fourteenth-century Vatican collection of Diatessaron texts in Vulgar Italian which includes examples in the widely used Tuscan and Venetian dialects. Some of these texts were employed in Church services, as they have the form of a lectionary. As noted in Chapter 2, the Italian linguistic experts consulted by the Raggs indicated a mixture of Venetian and Tuscan dialects in *Barnabas*. Slomp gives fourteen reasons why he thinks the gospel was an attempt at a harmony. The order of events in the Tuscan and Venetian Diatessaron and that of *Barnabas* is almost the same with reference to the birth and early ministry of Jesus. The same difficult words in both are left untranslated, and there are clusters of gospel texts combined in units of the same length and dealing with the same subjects. The date of the Tuscan and Venetian harmonies makes it possible for them to have been used by a 'Fra Marino'.

The idea of a gospel harmony also meets the Muslim demand that there was one original gospel. Harmonising the four Gospels might explain some of the geographical confusion we find in the document: there is a great deal of travelling back and forth from Jerusalem to Galilee – at times it is uncertain just where Jesus and his disciples are.[81]

Generally, *Barnabas* is not an easy 'read': it consists of approximately 75,000 words. (The Synoptic Gospels of Matthew, Mark and Luke are respectively 26,000, 17,000 and 28,000 words long; John 21,000 words long.) Despite its missionary tone, one wonders if the author had intended the work for popular consumption: only the most curious reader would plough through endless discourses and frequently repetitive rhetoric to be rewarded by some imaginative narrative and intricate reworking of the life of Jesus.

The author gives the work a lengthy title: *The True Gospel of Jesus, Called Christ, a New Prophet Sent by God to the World: According to the Description of Barnabas His Apostle.* The preface which follows, 'to all them that dwell upon the earth desireth peace and consolation', attacks Paul as among those who are deceived by Satan into preaching a 'most impious doctrine' by 'calling Jesus son of God, repudiating the circumcision ... and permitting every unclean meat'. Those were, as we have seen, the exact concerns of the Ebionites.

Barnabas' account of the nativity combines elements of Matthew's and Luke's stories with little variance, except that Mary was 'surrounded by a light exceeding bright' and brought forth her son 'without pain'. The latter touch, as we have noted, contradicts the Koran. As in the Venetian Diatessaron, the number of Magi is given; the carol 'We Three Kings' notwithstanding, Matthew only speaks of 'wise men' ('astrologers' in the *New English Bible*).

Like Luke's Gospel, *Barnabas* says that Jesus began his ministry when he was thirty years of age, but adds a strongly koranic note of having Jesus miraculously receiving 'the gospel' from the angel Gabriel. This is reminiscent of accounts in Suras 2 and 9 of the reception of revelation by Muhammad through the angel Gabriel.

In *Barnabas* Jesus goes to the Mount of Olives with his mother to gather olives. At noon, as he was praying, he is surrounded by an exceeding bright light and an infinite multitude of angels. The angel Gabriel presents him with a book, 'as it were a shining mirror', which descends into his heart; and he has knowledge of what God has said and wills.

Following the revelation, we have the first of many occasions when Jesus speaks privately to his apostle Barnabas: 'Believe, Barnabas, that I know every prophet with every prophecy, insomuch that whatever I say the whole hath come forth from that book.' Jesus then tells his mother that he must suffer 'great persecution for the honour of God' and can no longer live with her. Mary understands, and Jesus departs 'to attend to his prophetic office'.

Jesus goes to Jerusalem and makes a great impression upon the people by his preaching. 'The whole city was moved' by his words, and following a fast of forty days he chooses his twelve apostles which include Barnabas. In place of the canonical Gospels' Thomas and Simon Zealot we are told of the inclusion of Barnabas and Thaddaeus.

In Chapter 23 of *Barnabas*, Jesus gives a lengthy dissertation on the origin of circumcision and a condemnation of the uncircumcised which would please either a Muslim or a Jewish Christian reader. Chapters that follow continue important Muslim themes: the importance of Abraham, the role of his son Ishmael and a presentation of the Muslim profession of faith. Abraham, being neither Jew nor Christian, was the ideal figure symbolising a primitive, undistorted monotheism; and Muhammad, as the last of a succession of prophets, was the true heir of Abraham. *Barnabas* gives a version of the important koranic story of the young Abraham mocking and destroying the idols of Ur – in a sense, the symbolic beginning of monotheism.

Ishmael, son of Abraham by the slave girl Hagar, is equally important in Muslim tradition: the 'lesser pilgrimage' to Mecca commemorates Hagar's frantic search for water for her infant son; and Id al-Adha, the feast of the sacrifice, remembers Abraham's attempted sacrifice of Ishmael. Muslim tradition says that it was not the younger son, Isaac (offspring of Abraham's wife, Sarah) but Ishmael who was prepared for sacrifice. It is with these two sons that we find the divergence between the children of Abraham: the Jews through Isaac and the Arabs through Ishmael. The author of *Barnabas* has the Ishmael story frequently to the fore of his writing. Though the Koran does not actually name Ishmael as the intended victim (Sura 37), the account in *Barnabas* leaves us in no doubt: to its author the term 'Ishmaelite' becomes almost a synonym for 'Muslim'. *Barnabas* frequently displays the role of commentator on the Koran, making explicit what is implied. We shall see this tendency in fullest bloom with the Crucifixion account. There is little doubt in my mind that the author of the gospel was well acquainted either with commentaries on the Koran and/or popular Muslim tradition.

Chapter 39 contains the first of nine mentions of Muhammad by name as the prophet to follow Jesus; he is also referred to indirectly several times as the expected Messiah or as 'Messenger'. Jesus speaks of Adam's proclamation of a writing he saw 'that shone like the sun': 'There is only one God and Muhammad is the Messenger of God.' This is the first of the five pillars of Islam. God told Adam that Muhammad's soul was 'set in a celestial splendour 60,000 years before I made anything', and placed in writing on Adam's right thumbnail the words, 'There is only one God,' and on his left, 'Muhammad[82] is the messenger of God'.

The transfiguration follows, but only after Jesus has proclaimed, in the fashion of John the Baptist in the canonical Gospels, that one comes after him 'the ties of the hosen or the latchets of the shoes' he is not worthy to unloose. He is the Messiah: as noted earlier, *Barnabas* goes against the Koran in ascribing this title to Muhammad and seems unaware that the term 'Christ' which he

38

uses means the same thing. In discussing the lineage of this Messiah, the author of *Barnabas* insists that 'the promise was made in Ishmael', not in Isaac as the Jews insist.

Chapter 70 contains a good example of how the author of *Barnabas* has rewritten for his own purposes an important Gospel account, namely Peter's proclamation at Caesarea Philippi that Jesus is the Son of God. After Jesus has asked what men say of him, the disciples respond as in Matthew 16.13ff that some say he is Elijah, others Jeremiah or one of the other prophets (John the Baptist's name is omitted as elsewhere in *Barnabas*, as if he had never existed). Peter answers that he is the Son of God. In Matthew, Jesus rejoices: 'Simon, ... you are favoured indeed! You did not learn that from mortal man; it was revealed to you by my heavenly Father.' In the *Barnabas* account Jesus is angry at the confession and rebukes Peter, saying, 'Begone and depart from me because thou art a devil and seekest to cause me offense.' He threatens the others: 'Woe to you if you believe this, for I have won from God a great curse against those who believe this.' Jesus' anger continues, and he 'was fain to cast away Peter', but the others restrain him and he rebukes him again, saying, 'Beware that never again thou say such words, because God will reprobate thee.' Peter weeps and prays for God's forgiveness for having spoken so foolishly. Jesus then departs into Galilee 'in order that this vain opinion which the common folk began to hold concerning him might be extinguished'.

Shortly after this, Jesus warns the disciples of what befalls them because of their association with him. *Barnabas* notes that already Judas 'had hand with the priests, and reported to them all that Jesus spake'. Again, Jesus speaks specially to Barnabas – 'he who writeth this' – and Barnabas asks who will betray him. Jesus responds that the answer to that question cannot yet be given.

There are in *Barnabas* a number of parables not to be found in the canonical Gospels, and one taken from Chapter 76 will give an idea of how the author of this gospel used his considerable imagination (and/or possibly now lost sources) to imitate the well-known examples. *Barnabas*' story of the cultivation of vineyards is in part reminiscent of Matthew's parable of the wicked farmers (21.33–43) and Luke's parable of the talents (19.11–27); yet the general tone is original.

A man with three vineyards lets them out to three husbandmen. The first does not know how to cultivate his vines and brings forth only leaves. The second teaches the way the vines ought to be cultivated to the third, who learns so well that his vines bear much fruit; however, the former leaves his own vineyard uncultivated, spending his time talking. When the time comes for paying rent, the first husbandman tells the lord of the vineyard that he has no fruit as he did not know how to cultivate his vineyard.

The lord is not pleased and inquires why he had not asked the second husbandman for advice. He is tempted to throw him into prison until the debt is paid, but is moved to pity because of 'his simplicity'. The second man – the one who knows the art of vine-dressing – complains his vineyard is backward. The lord calls to account the third man, who says that he has learned well from the second husbandman about vine-dressing. The lord then asks why the second man's vineyard has not borne fruit. The third answers that 'the vines are not cultivated by talking only, but he needs must sweat a shirt every day who willeth to make it bring forth its fruit': he should 'put into practice his own words'. The lord is angry with the second man and has him 'beaten without any mercy'. Matters do not end there: 'And then he put him into prison under the keeping of a cruel servant who beat him every day, and never was willing to set him free for prayers of his friends.' The presentation of God's justice at the end is a step more harsh than what one usually finds in the canonical Gospels.

Chapter 91 – the chapter of 'the great tumult' – is among the most chimerical of the accounts to be found in *Barnabas*: 'At this time there was a great disturbance throughout Judaea for the sake of Jesus: for that the Roman soldiery, through the operation of Satan, stirred up the Hebrews, saying that Jesus was God come to visit them.' So great a sedition arises that for forty days 'all Judaea was in arms'. In order to quieten the people it is necessary that the high priest should ride in procession, clothed in his priestly robes with the tetragrammaton (the holy name of God) on his forehead; in like manner ride the governor and Herod. At Mizpah, armies of 200,000 men assemble.[83] Herod speaks to them, but they are not quietened. Then Pilate and the high priest say: 'Brethren, this war is aroused by the work of Satan, for Jesus is alive, and to him we ought to resort, and ask him that he give testimony of himself, and then believe in him, according to his word.' At this the soldiers become calm and embrace one another, asking for forgiveness. The three leaders, having stilled the rebellion, will have to deal with Jesus later. *Barnabas* assumes that Roman soldiers were involved in the intricate theological discussions of the Jews and that large numbers of them were influenced by Jesus' preaching.

Jesus returns to Jerusalem after spending forty days with his disciples at Mount Sinai! This period is referred to as 'the forty days', as if Lent had been observed at that time – another of the minor tell-tale slips made by the author. Upon his return, the word spreads that 'Our God cometh': the people go out 'everyone, small and great, to see Jesus, insomuch that the city was left empty.' The scene makes the canonical Gospel account a minor event by comparison. Again, we have the arch-enemies Pilate, Herod and the high priest acting as close companions as they decide to find Jesus 'that the sedition of the people might be quieted'. They discover him in the wilderness near the Jordan.

Jesus marvels at 'the multitude which covered the ground with people', and says to his disciples: 'Perchance Satan hath raised sedition in Judaea. May it please God to take away from Satan the dominion which he hath over sinners.' The crowds draw nearer and begin to cry out, 'Welcome to thee, O Our God!'; they do him reverence 'as unto God'. Jesus gives 'a great groan' and says, 'Get ye from before me, O madmen.' The people are filled with terror and begin to weep. A very long confession follows, with Jesus protesting that he is not God: 'I am Jesus, son of Mary' [the expression used in the Koran] ... of the seed of David, a man that is mortal and feareth God.'

The high priest reminds Jesus that the Book of Moses says that God will send a Messiah, and asks if that is he. Jesus answers that he is not. Caiaphas, Pilate and Herod (again in cahoots) tell the people they will write 'the sacred Roman Senate in such wise that by imperial decree none shall any more call thee God or son of God'. Jesus is 'not consoled' by these words and proceeds, again in John-the-Baptist-fashion, to foretell the coming of the messenger of God: 'Muhammad is his blessed name.'

The finale of this extraordinary episode is the crowd lifting up their voices saying: 'O God, send us thy messenger: O Muhammad, come quickly for the salvation of the world!' The high priest asks Pilate to write to Rome, which he does; and the Senate 'had compassion on Israel and decreed that on pain of death none should call Jesus ... either God or son of God'. The decree engraved upon copper is posted up in the temple.

After this flight of fancy, *Barnabas* returns to canonical Gospel material with the well-known story of the feeding of the five thousand – a few faithful left over from the multitudes described earlier proclaiming him God! Long sections follow with discussions of prayer and fasting which are evocative of medieval monastic discipline – and they are admirably presented. Here *Barnabas* moves away from polemics and we see a welcome depth of spirituality. This mood is broken in Chapter 112, where Jesus talks privately to the apostle Barnabas ('All the disciples and apostles departed by fours and sixes and went their way') but there remains 'he who writeth' to whom Jesus unburdens his soul, declaring, 'O Barnabas, it is necessary that I should reveal to thee great secrets.' The secrets include the statement that he will be sold by one of his disciples for thirty pieces of money and that that person will be slain in his name: 'God shall take me up from the earth, and shall change the appearance of the traitor so everyone shall believe him to be me.' This infamy will remain until Muhammad comes and then the truth will be known.

There follow long discussions of the judgement day and hell. *Barnabas'* description of the latter is similar to the vividness of the koranic view in Sura 22. *Barnabas* has 'raging hunger, burning flames, scorching cinders, and cruel torments with bitter weeping', while the Koran tells us: 'Garments of fire have been prepared for the unbelievers. Scalding water shall be poured upon their heads, melting their skins and that which is in their bellies. They shall be lashed with rods of iron.' In the gospel, Muhammad is presented as the enemy of devils: 'When he shall go there all the devils shall shriek, and seek to hide themselves beneath the burning embers, saying one to another: "Fly, fly, for here cometh Muhammad our enemy!"'

In Chapter 152, Judas confers with the priests. He has 'lost hope of becoming powerful in the world ... he had hoped Jesus would become King of Israel, and so he himself would be a powerful man'. Judas plots to deliver Jesus to the authorities. Jesus and his disciples happen to be in Damascus at this time! They return to Galilee.

Chapter 192 offers another clue as to the authorship of the gospel. It speaks of an 'old book written by the hand of Moses and Joshua ... Therein is written that Ishmael is the father of the Messiah.' According to Jan Slomp, the author of *Barnabas* 'tried to take revenge upon the former inquisitor in Venice, Pope Sixtus V, by recounting the finding of the Gospel of Barnabas in the papal library'.[84] There is an interesting connection between the account in Chapter 192 and the Fra Marino story (see page 9). In the former, we have the discovery of a so far hidden true book of Moses by Nicodemus in the temple (read 'Vatican', as Slomp suggests). The high priest (read 'pope') did not allow Nicodemus (that is, the author of *Barnabas*) to see it because it was supposed to have been written by an Ishmaelite (that is, a Muslim). According to Slomp, these remarks 'give the author away'. The author of *Barnabas* was 'hiding behind the high priest in Chapter 192 – that is behind Pope Sixtus V'. As noted in the next chapter, this possibility has a great bearing on the authorship question.

Jesus enters Jerusalem for the last time in Chapter 200, and we have the beginning of *Barnabas*' peculiar Passion narrative. The Palm Sunday episode is now completely overshadowed by the previous demonstrations in Jerusalem for Jesus: the scene is rather anticlimactic. Jesus enters the temple and is immediately confronted by the scribes and Pharisees on the matter of a woman taken in adultery. This is the account from John's Gospel which was traditionally placed as John 7.53-8.11 but which in the *New English Bible* was removed from the main body of the Gospel and placed at the end because the editors found in the ancient accounts 'no fixed position'. It is odd that the author of *Barnabas* puts the story towards the end of his gospel – probably just a coincidence in his general rearranging of material.

Jesus is interrogated by the high priest as to his identity in the several chapters which follow, and in the final episode he angers the priest by saying that the son of Abraham whom he was willing to sacrifice was Ishmael, not Isaac and that the Messiah was descended from the son of Hagar, not that of Sarah. Caiaphas cries out: 'Let us stone this impious fellow, for he is an Ishmaelite, and hath spoken blasphemy against Moses and against the law of God!' 'Every scribe and Pharisee with the elders of the people took up stones to stone Jesus', but he vanishes from their sight and leaves the temple.

Mary is prepared for what will happen to her son by the angel Gabriel. She is told that Jesus will be protected from the world and that she will not be able to see him any more in the world 'save after the deed of shame for that the angel Gabriel, with the angels Michael, Raphael, and Uriel will bring him to her'.

Again the high priest, Pilate and Herod are together deciding what to do with Jesus. Pilate says they have 'an ill venture' in their hands, for if they slay Jesus they will have acted in a manner that is contrary to the decree of Caesar (in a second decree, it was forbidden that anyone 'should contend concerning Jesus of Nazareth'). Herod threatens to accuse Pilate before Caesar of being a rebel unless he does something; and Pilate, fearing the senate, makes friends with him. The others tell the high priest they will send soldiers to search for Jesus.

43

Jesus consoles his disciples in the house of Nicodemus and following a lengthy prayer as to his true intentions, we have *Barnabas'* account of the last supper. It has many of the elements of the canonical Gospel presentations without, of course, the account of the institution of the Eucharist.

Judas betrays Jesus for thirty pieces of gold ('silver' in the New Testament) and 'draws near to the place where Jesus was'. God sees 'the danger of his servant' and commands Gabriel 'to take Jesus out of the world'. In the Koran, following the denial of Jesus' death on the cross, it is said 'Allah lifted him up to His presence' (4.158), in *Barnabas*, the angels take Jesus 'out by the window that looketh toward the South'. He is placed in 'the third heaven in the company of angels blessing God for evermore'.

As the narrative continues, Judas 'impetuously enters before all into the chamber whence Jesus had been taken up'. The disciples are asleep, 'whereupon the wonderful God acted wonderfully, insomuch that Judas was so changed in speech and in face to be like Jesus that we believed him to be Jesus'. What is implied in Sura 4.156ff of the Koran is portrayed graphically and drawn out in an almost ludicrous fashion in *Barnabas*. The literal translation given by Dawood for Sura 4.156ff is: 'They did not kill him, nor did they crucify him, but *he was made to resemble another for them*.' We shall see in Chapter 6 that the discussion of this passage is a highly complicated and controversial matter; but generally koranic commentators have offered a substitution for Jesus on the cross. The eighth-century Arabian storyteller Wahb offered an account similar to what is presented in *Barnabas*: there is the betrayal of Jesus by Judas, the trial, and the preparation of the cross; then a cloud of darkness comes down, God sends angels to protect Jesus, and Judas is crucified in his place. This is cited by Tabari, who also suggests in another writing that a Jewish chief named Joshua is changed into Jesus' form and appearance and crucified in his place despite his own protests.[85]

In the manuscript of Abd al-Jabbar discussed in Chapter 1 we saw a Crucifixion presentation from an unknown gospel which, to Jabbar's delight, vindicates the koranic doctrine of the mistaken Crucifixion; as noted earlier Jabbar erroneously believed the account to be from the canonical Gospels. In the story, Judas had promised to single out his Master by kissing him but kisses the wrong man. The man's perturbed reactions are similar to those of Judas in *Barnabas*.[86]

As the Passion narrative continues in *Barnabas*, Judas is

surprised that the disciples think he is Jesus: 'And he, smiling, said: "Now are ye foolish, that know not me to be Judas Iscariot."' The drama continues with the soldiers arresting Judas. The disciples flee, and there is another interesting side-touch here. Mark 14.51 states that a young man 'with nothing on but a linen cloth' is among those following Jesus. There is an attempt to seize him – 'but he slipped out of the linen cloth and ran away naked'. Some authorities identify him as John Mark, the evangelist and cousin of St. Barnabas, and this is also the case in *Barnabas*, where he is called John. Judas is bound by the soldiers and flogged. He continues to protest the mistake which has been made and is thought to be 'feigning madness'. He is interrogated by the high priest and later 'attired as a juggler and so treated ... that it would have moved the very Canaanites to compassion if they had beheld that sight'.

The account of Judas before Pilate is suggestive of those in the canonical Gospels, but with the former strongly protesting his innocence: 'Sir, believe me, if thou put me to death, thou shalt do a great wrong, for thou shalt slay an innocent person; seeing that I am Judas Iscariot, and not Jesus, who is a magician, and by his art hath so transformed me.' Pilate 'marvels greatly' at his words and says that if what he protests is true it would be a great wrong to kill him. The chief priests, elders, scribes and Pharisees will have none of this, and claim if he goes free a 'sedition will stir'. As in Luke, Pilate reminds them that Jesus is a Galilean and should therefore be tried by Herod. After being questioned, and 'clad in white as fools are clad', Judas is sent back to Pilate. Herod sends word to Pilate that he should 'not fail in justice to the people of Israel'. According to *Barnabas*, Herod wrote this 'because the chief priests, scribes and Pharisees had given him a good quantity of money. The governor having heard that this was so from a servant of Herod, in order that he also might gain some money, feigned that he desired to set Judas at liberty'.

Pilate causes Judas to be scourged 'by his slaves who were paid by the scribes to slay him under the scourges'. *Barnabas* adds that this is not to be his death for 'God ... had decreed the issue, reserved Judas for the cross, in order that he might suffer that horrible death to which he had sold another'. Judas does not die under the scourges 'notwithstanding that the soldiers scourged him so grievously that his body rained blood'. He is next clothed in purple and crowned with a crown of thorns, as in the canonical Passion.

The chief priests, scribes and Pharisees, seeing that Judas did not die by the scourging and fearing that Pilate will set him free, 'made a gift of money to the governor', who then turns Judas over for crucifixion. *Barnabas* states that he was crucified 'naked for the greater ignominy'. The only words from Judas on the cross are, 'God, why hast thou forsaken me, seeing the malefactor hath escaped and I die unjustly?' *Barnabas* says 'the voice, the face, and the person of Judas were so like to Jesus, that his disciples and believers entirely believed that he was Jesus; whereupon some departed from the doctrine of Jesus, believing that Jesus had been a false prophet'. As we shall see, the chief reason Muslims cannot accept the Crucifixion of Isa (Jesus) the prophet is that Allah would not allow 'the accursed death' for one of his true prophets.

Judas is buried in Joseph's new sepulchre as in the canonical Gospels, having been wrapped up 'in an hundred pounds of precious ointment'. The disciples go to their homes, and Barnabas, John and James go with Mary to Nazareth (in John's Gospel, it is 'the disciple whom he loved' who takes her 'into his home'). News reaches them in Nazareth that there is a rumour that Jesus has risen from the dead, and Mary wants to return to Jerusalem to find her son: 'I shall die content when I have seen him.' The high priest has commanded all, 'under pain of anathema, that no one shall talk of Jesus of Nazareth'.

The angels 'that were guardians of Mary' ascend to the third heaven and recount to Jesus all that has happened. Jesus prays to God that he have power to see his mother and disciples. The koranic commentator Tabari has Jesus descending from heaven to Mary and his disciples after she has has prayed at the foot of the cross for seven days (with the transformed 'Joshua' still there). In *Barnabas*, Jesus is borne by the archangels to his mother's house and tells Mary and his disciples what actually happened: 'Believe me, mother, for verily I say to thee that I have not been dead at all; for God hath reserved me till near the end of the world.' There are a number of Islamic traditions which assert that in the last days Jesus will descend in the Holy Land, kill the Antichrist (*al-Dajjal*) and go to Jerusalem, where he will worship, kill swine and slay all who do not believe in him, then reign in peace for forty years and finally die and be buried in Medina beside the tomb of Muhammad. These traditions, are, of course, a great elaboration on what in the Koran are merely hints.

Barnabas has Jesus asking the archangels testify that what he has told his mother is the truth. The testimonial involves Jesus giving 'four linen cloths to the angels that they might cover themselves in order that they might be seen and heard to speak by his mother and her companions'. The following scene has Barnabas ('he who writeth') asking a question which must have been anticipated by the gospel's author as he concocted his elaborate Passion scenario: 'seeing that God is merciful, wherefore hath he so tormented us, making us believe that thou wert dead?' Barnabas adds that Mary 'hath so wept for thee that she hath been nigh to death'.

Jesus' answer is not terribly convincing. Though he has been 'innocent in the world since men have called me "God", and "Son of God", God, in order that I be not mocked of the demons on the day of judgement, hath willed that I be mocked of men in this world by the death of Judas, making all men to believe that I died upon the cross'. Again Jesus reminds his faithful that 'this mocking shall continue until the advent of Muhammad, the messenger of God, who, when he shall come, shall reveal this deception to those who believe in God's law'. This polemical rationalisation is but one of the many the author of the gospel has created for himself by reworking and rewriting material from the canonical Gospels. The modern reader of *Barnabas* continues to plough through its many pages for no other reason than to see how the writer is going to overcome some of the obstacles he has set in his path. The end result is the same in some of the apocryphal gospels and in all of the 'modern' ones: the writing is forced to fit a preconceived design. Whether it be *The Passover Plot*[87] or the Ahmadiyya Muslim scenarios, we end up with more problems and questions than were ever presented by the material of the canonical Gospels.

Jesus turns to Barnabas in the penultimate chapter of the gospel and charges that 'by all means thou write my gospel concerning all that hath happened through my dwelling in the world. And write in like manner that which hath befallen Judas, in order that the faithful may be undeceived, and every one may believe the truth'. The ascension occurs three days later (according to Acts 1.3, it happened forty days after the Resurrection), and Jesus' last words make certain the disciples know the truth: 'Verily I say unto you, I died not, but Judas the traitor. Beware, for Satan will make every effort to deceive you, but be ye my witnesses in all Israel, and throughout the world.'

The last chapter is similar to the first in attacking Paul, and the author says that after Jesus had departed:

the truth, hated of Satan, was persecuted, as it always is, by falsehood. For certain evil men, pretending to be disciples, preached that Jesus died and rose not again. Others preached that

47

he really died, but rose again. Others preached, and yet preach, that Jesus is the Son of God, among whom Paul is deceived. But we, as much as I have written, that preach we to those who fear God, that they may be saved in the last day of God's Judgement. Amen.[88]

CHAPTER FOUR

The Authorship of *Barnabas*: Just Who Was Fra Marino?

In Britain in the 1970s there appeared a series of comic strip books that centred around another 'Barnabas': the humorous creation of Graham Jeffery. In the first of the books, Jeffery has a portly and monkish-looking Barnabas approaching the evangelist John and asking, 'Excuse me, John. Do you mind if I write a gospel too?'

John turns from his writing-desk and answers, 'Of course not, Barnabas. Everybody should write a gospel.' He continues, 'Matthew's written one and he used to be a tax-collector ... Luke's written one giving the medical angle ... and young Mark's written one. And hundreds of others who never got them printed. But that doesn't matter because Jesus is still alive and doing things today, and if you were to write down all the things Jesus did you'd never get all the books onto the world. Besides – if only one person read and enjoyed your gospel it wouldn't be wasted.'

Barnabas smiles and looks over at John. 'Do you mean that if only *one* person reads my gospel it won't be wasted?' He walks away anxious to begin. 'If the worst comes to the worst, I can always read it myself.'[89]

I do not know whether or not Graham Jeffery was aware that a spurious gospel attributed to Barnabas actually existed when he created his 'Barnabas'. Anyway, the foregoing can be seen as a delightfully unconscious discussion of the authorship of the Vienna manuscript: 'If the worst comes to the worst, I can always read it myself.' For whom was *Barnabas* intended – and just who was the writer?

Qazi Muhammad Hafizullah wrote in his preface to the 1981 edition: 'If we accept it as a forgery, as the Christian scholars say, then the most surprising fact which baffles explanation is how a man of such remarkable and superb talents who forged this Gospel has remained unknown to this day.'[90]

As we have seen, there is overwhelming evidence that Codex 2662 is a medieval production: the handwriting, paper and its watermark alone are enough to decide the issue for any museum. The internal evidence is equally decisive: the tell-tale clues given in the 'Jubilee Year' and 'true book of Moses' episodes (see pages 29 and 43–4); a medieval Italian flavour to much of the writing; spectacular geographical and historical errors no first-century Palestinian writer could have made; and the enthusiasm of a 'convert' which sometimes make *Barnabas* more Muslim than the Koran.[91]

When *The Gospel of Barnabas* first appeared on the historical scene in Amsterdam at the beginning of the eighteenth century, there was speculation that its existence had been known of earlier. John Toland spoke of the 'Gospel never publicly made known among Christians though they have much talked about the Muslims acknowledging the Gospel;[92] and in his dedicatory preface to the manuscript as presented to Prince Eugene, J. F. Cramer wrote: 'no Christian was allowed to see it, although they strove with all means at their disposal to find it and take a look at it'.[93]

Sale in his *Preliminary Discourse* commented: 'The Mohammedans have also a Gospel in Arabic, attributed to St. Barnabas.'[94] This remark gave rise to a barrage of speculation that an Arabic original existed. Later, in the preface to his translation of the Koran, Sale admitted that he had not seen an Arabic edition but was merely repeating the conjecture given by two other writers, John Toland and Bernard de la Monnoye (see page 26). Al-Haj Khwaja Nazir Ahmad proposes that Sale made a 'wicked suggestion' in attributing the origin of the gospel to the Muslims, and he makes a point of what he calls Sale's 'confession'.[95] A number of eighteenth-century writers assumed that an Arabic original existed, and a number of Muslim authors followed the suggestion. Almost all the speculation can be traced back to Sale's unfortunate remark. As the Raggs write in their introduction, the discussion of an Arabic original was the mere supposition of some Christian scholars and

'Muslim controversalists, who, though challenged again and again during nearly two centuries, have never yet produced a copy of *Barnabas* in Arabic and are believed to owe their knowledge of the "Gospel's" existence to the writings of George Sale, which they certainly possess.'[96] The numerous red ink Arabic glosses in the margins of the Italian manuscript have been a part of the 'Arabic original' discussion. They are reminiscent of koranic phrases, but curiously, as with the entire manuscript, contain no direct quotations from the Muslim holy book. According to the study by Cirillo and Frémaux,[97] they present so many dissonant elements that no orthodox Muslim could have written them. Cirillo also thinks it possible that they were influenced by Turkish, which might add something to the Raggs' observation that the dark green binding of the manuscript 'has an almost precise counterpart in the binding of a Turkish document of 1575' kept in the Venetian archives. It is not known whether the binding was original; if it is the work of Prince Eugene's Parisian binders, it is, according to the Raggs, 'an astonishingly faithful copy of oriental models'.[98] According to my own observation of it there is a clear impression of the binding being original, and perhaps this is a clue to the creation of the manuscript: as the example the Raggs cited, it could also have been bound in Constantinople—to add another 'original touch' to the creation.

Unfortunately, the historical appearance of *Barnabas* in Amsterdam in the eighteenth century is abrupt even if we accept that Gregorio Leti brought it there from Italy. Despite its fanciful nature, it seems to me that the Spanish preface's story of 'Fra Marino' and Pope Sixtus V is the natural starting-point for discussing the authorship of *Barnabas*, and it is surprising what little examination there has been on this point. The search for a historical Fra Marino takes us into an intriguing world and uncovers some fascinating possibilities. There are any number of accounts of renegade monks of the Middle Ages. The editor of the Indian journal *Epiphany*, in an article later reprinted in the 1923 *Moslem World*, mentions an example also to be found in the Raggs' introduction: 'the notorious Fra Vincenzo Marini, who after a series of adventurous frauds was claimed, when already condemned to the galleys, by the Inquisitor in Venice, on a charge of apostasy'.[99] Centuries earlier, Philip the Fair, in his desire to lay hands on the wealth of the Knights Templar, found an accomplice in an apostate Italian Templar; and there were any number of charges against the order that members had gone over to the infidel. Lonsdale Ragg entertained the possibility that the author 'may have been one of the apostate Templars'.[100]

Jan Slomp's analysis of the 'Jubilee Year' passage (see page 29) is attractive and is for me further confirmation for placing the gospel's creation in the time of Sixtus V. There are a number of indications from the biographies of Sixtus V which make it feasible that he was the 'sleeping Pontiff in the library'.

Sixtus V was born Felice Peretti in 1520, at Grottammare near Montalto in the Italian Marches. He was the son of a labourer and entered a Franciscan monastery in 1533. His ability as a preacher attracted the attention of Cardinal Carpi, the protector of the Franciscans, who brought him to Rome in 1552. There again he attracted the attention of influential clergy, the future popes Cardinal Carafa (Paul IV) and Cardinal Ghislieri (Pius V). In 1557 the former appointed him father inquisitor of the Venetian republic, where he also served as rector of the Franciscan order and director of studies.

Peretti was not liked either by members of his order or by the citizens of Venice. He was a foreigner in a position previously held by clergy from the immediate area. Ludwig Von Pastor sees the origin of opposition to Peretti in the Franciscan convent itself. Peretti was condemned for his excessive severity and notable ambition. Gregorio Leti's condemned biography states that he took revenge against members of his order, and that point at least is substantiated by other writers[101]. Von Pastor says:

> It is not surprising that he should have had a reputation of that kind, since his superior had already on many occasions charged him with the reform of the convents of the Conventual Franciscans, his ecclesiastical zeal had found many things that called for improvement. By nature very brusque and violent, his intervention repeatedly led to much discontent. The adversaries of Fra Felice grew in numbers.[102]

It was also objected against Peretti that he published the Index of Paul IV prematurely in Venice. From 1549 to 1559 publishers resisted papal attempts to impose an Index of Prohibited Books on the Venetian press, the most influential in all of Italy, which in the sixteenth century produced half or more of all books printed on the peninsula. Their record, portrayed with competence by Paul Grendler,[103] is a remarkable story of tension between the papacy and the republic. At the end of the 1540s the government of Venice moved to draft an Index of Prohibited Books, as had been done earlier in Milan and Siena. The catalogue of forbidden books printed in 1549 banned forty-seven authors, most of them northern Protestants, as well as bibles with prefaces and glosses attacking the Catholic faith. The papal nuncio, Giovanni Della Casa, sent a manuscript copy of the catalogue to Rome, lamenting that after the great labour involved in the production of the document its promulgation was not assured. The opposition to the 1549 ban in Venice noted that no such Index existed in Rome – where every sort of book was sold publicly. The catalogue was suppressed, and though a new attempt was made in 1554-5, this was later withdrawn. The Venetian Holy Office of the Inquisition then resorted to individual decrees, especially with the arrival of Peretti. Peretti's friend Cardinal Carafa was elected pope in 1555 and was a great foe of heretical literature. He had another Index in mind, and it is possible that he withdrew the 1554 version so as to prepare his cardinals to produce a far stronger one.

The Holy Office advised bookmen in 1558 that they were forbidden to print the Bible in any vernacular, and decreed that anyone importing books into Venice had to deposit an inventory with the Office before they could clear customs. Although local Indices had been issued across Europe, it was not until 1559 that Rome, under Paul IV, published the first general *Index Librorum Prohibitorum*. The pope's Index was an undiscriminating list which included all the works of Erasmus and all translations of the Bible into vernacular language; it also reflected the puritanical character of Counter-Reformation censorship. Books were judged not only as heretical but also as anticlerical, immoral, lascivious or obscene. Grendler writes: 'In Paul IV's Rome, where even cardinals held their tongues for fear of the Inquisition, the new Index produced great consternation and caused large numbers of books to be destroyed.'[104]

Paul IV had in Venice a cleric who would carry out his new designs, but Peretti met strong resistance to the new decree: bookmen would not print the Index or submit inventories to the Holy Office. Grendler relates that on learning of the situation in Venice, 'the Dominican grand inquisitor, Cardinal Ghislieri, 'exploded in rage. It was monstrous that the Index could not be printed and promulgated in a Catholic city under a most Catholic prince!'[105]

Peretti pushed for implementation in such a manner he received

53

the ire of Venetian patricians. Grendler says that 'as he was entering the room in the ducal palace ... a member of the Dona family spat in his face'.[106] On the death of Paul IV in 1559, Peretti fled Venice and retired to Montalto. A former patron, Cardinal Carpi, learned with great indignation of the affronts to his former protégé. Carpi persuaded the new pope, Pius V, to reinstate Peretti in February of the following year with even greater powers both as father inquisitor and director of studies for the Franciscans. Von Pastor says:

'Fra Felice's adversaries, headed by the superior of the Franciscan convent, were extremely angry at this. They accused him before the Council of Ten, and the latter, always jealous to uphold the claims of the state, was easily won over. In the meantime the matter had been referred to the Congregation of the Inquisition in Rome. They decided upon the recall of Fra Felice, but at the same time took away the Inquisition from the Franciscans and gave it to the Dominicans. In the end, the members of the Franciscan convent, with the exception of the fanatical superior, came to their senses, but it was too late to undo the harm which had been done to the order. At the end of June 1560, Fra Felice left Venice in the same year the Roman Inquisition had appointed him its consultor.[107]

Baron Hubner's biography minimises the less attractive side of Sixtus V's character, and relates that Peretti

had the extreme generosity to propose for the vacant place of superior of his order the monk who had been his most active and pitiless antagonist at Venice. This was much remarked at the time, and still more so when, soon afterwards, the new superior, condemned for various offenses, was summoned to Rome to undergo his punishment, Fra Felice interceded for him, and obtained from the Holy Father his pardon. This act of Christian herosim was specially noticed and appreciated by Cardinal Ghislieri (later to be Pius V)'.[108]

With the death of Gregory XIII in 1585, the Sacred College of Cardinals was divided by rival factions, and Peretti emerged as the new pope. His short pontificate of five years was marked by energy and forcefulness. Sixtus V cracked down on clerical discipline and had the severed heads of local bandits exhibited on the Sant' Angelo bridge. He created new tribunals of the Inquisition, ordered a new Index and had his favourite architect, Domenico Fontana, move the great obelisk of Caligula to its present site in front of St. Peter's as well as build the new Vatican library. Sixtus V was fascinated by books, and it is said that he had nearly two dozen prohibited titles in his large personal library. Grendler comments: 'The catholicity of the banned titles and, indeed, of his entire library suggests that Peretti acquired prohibited works for personal and scholarly reasons'.[109]

One of Sixtus V's last achievements was the enormous task of preparing a revised edition of St. Jerome's translation of the Bible. As Grendler says, 'his enthusiasm exceeded his scholarship';[110] he impatiently set aside the scholarship of experts and handled much of the editorial work himself. In the spring of 1590 he set forth the result of his work as not only official but unalterable; so marred was it that his successor, Clement VIII, later had to recover as many copies as possible and issue a revised edition with more than 3,000 corrections. The following August he died, and in the words of Ivor Flower Burton: 'Posterity ranks Sixtus one of the greatest popes. He was hasty, severe, autocratic; but his mind was open to large ideas, and he threw himself into his undertakings with an energy and determination that often compelled success.'[111]

Sixtus V's successes were achieved at the price of making many enemies. There would have been any number of individuals seeking revenge on him; any number who might have wanted to link his name with a creation that proclaimed a truth contrary to his hated authoritarianism – perhaps a gospel capable of undermining the entire structure he had achieved with such singular determination, and a gospel to be found in his own personal library. The motive is not difficult to find – but the author?[112]

Lonsdale and Laura Ragg sought an exact identification of 'Fra Marino' in the Venetian archives. They came across a tempting choice with 'the notorious Fra Vincenzo Marini' mentioned earlier in this chapter, but they note that he was not born until 1573. The editor of *Epiphany* incorrectly dated his misadventures as 1549. Doubtless he confused Marini with the candidate the Raggs referred to previously: 'The name Marino, Marini, figures very frequently in Venetian annals; but the only contemporary friar of that name whom we have noted is a certain *Maestro Marino dell' ordine di S. Francesco*, who was responsible for an Index of prohibited books published in 1549.'[113]

I followed the Raggs' lead for a Venetian Franciscan Fra Marino when on a trip to Venice in 1982, and was told at the main public library that they possessed the only known copy of the 1549 catalogue of condemned books. They promised to send me a copy of the title page, and upon my return to London I discovered that the historian Horatio Brown had mentioned the same document in his *Studies in the History of Venice* (1907).[114] Paul Grendler says of Brown's find that it 'has been completely ignored by scholars'[115] and had for a long time been miscatalogued. The title-page said in part: 'Composed by the Reverend Father Maestro MARINO the Venetian, of the monastery of Friars Minor of Venice, of the conventual order of Saint Francis; Inquisitor.' Brown's two-volume work was published in 1907, the same year as the Raggs' translation of *Barnabas*, and it is not known whether or not the latter authors took note of his writing later on. Fra Marino as the father inquisitor of Venice added a considerable dimension to the discussion of the authorship of *Barnabas*, and I was glad to check my enthusiasm for this possibility by going through Grendler's sources. Two brief mentions whetted my appetite, and one in particular: 'Padre Marin(o) twice gave testimony to the Holy Office [of the Inquisition] in Venice, 9 August 1555, on matters concerning his term as inquisitor, 1542–50.' I promptly ordered the source, Busta (Case) 12 from the Santo Uffizio (Holy Office) materials in the Venetian archives.[116]

The file consists of forty-six pages under the general cover page of 'Padre Marin da Venezia'. The spelling presents no difficulty: frequently 'Marino' is written without the final 'o', and sometimes with a final 'i' instead of 'o'. Almost all the references in Busta 12 use the 'Marino' spelling as on the 1549 *Catalogo* title-page. As the Raggs say, Marino is a common name and usually a first name: Marin(o) Falier(o) (1285–1355) was immortalised in a tragic history by Lord Byron; Marino Marini was a gifted sculptor in this century. In private correspondence, Paul Grendler has suggested Marino was the inquisitor's first name, his surname being that of a Venetian nobleman. Like many Venetian clergy, he may have been illegitimate. As a surname, 'Marino' is listed by Stanley Chojnacki among the 244 patrician families of medieval Venice.[117]

The Cambridge Dante scholar Gavin N. Ryan helped me weed through the Holy Office file. It was a tiring task because the material consists of loose, unpaginated documents frequently in illegible and stained writing. Despite this, one receives an interesting picture of the Inquisition trials and the character of Fra Marino. At this time the Holy Office met regularly every Tuesday,

Thursday and Saturday, with few missed or altered dates. According to Grendler, the meeting-place in summer was the small church of San Teodoro, which was contiguous to the great basilica of San Marco; in winter, they assembled in a Franciscan presbytery until the father inquisitor was appointed from the Dominican order.[118] Trials began either with questioning of additional witnesses or with the initial interrogation of the accused who could name his personal witnesses. The father inquisitor systematically questioned the accused and normally did not reveal the full extent of the charge immediately – the heart of the inquisitional procedure was shrewd and persistent interrogation.

Busta 12 contains fifteen or so separate documents which deal directly or indirectly with Fra Marino. Much of the material consists of transcriptions of statements Marino and others made to the court, and unfortunately these are interspersed with matters not immediately concerned with the former inquisitor. One gets the impression that the Holy Office took a long time to get down to the real problems at hand. The few dated documents indicate that Marino appeared before the court on at least three separate occasions: 14 June 1555; 9 August 1555 and some time in the year 1561. Marino's term of office, 1542–50, was a longer one than the usual five-year period, and his last appearance before the Inquisition was after Fra Peretti had left Venice.

The general impression given by Marino's testimony is that of a former official greatly on the defensive concerning his handling of his office. Marino was viewed as having been too lenient – especially with those suspected of 'Lutheran' leanings. The term was used loosely by the Holy Office, but according to the Venetian state archives there were in the sixteenth century 803 inquisitional trials for 'Lutherans' compared with five for 'Calvinists', thirty-five for 'Anabaptists', sixty-five for blasphemous speech and 148 for sorcery. At the court appearance on 9 August 1555, Marino protests: 'I had an infinite number of heretical books burned; I made many theologians believe whether they were deserving of fire or not.' The former inquisitor also states that he 'does not have a distinct memory' concerning the details of some of the materials which came to his attention.

The papal nuncio to Venice, Giovanni Della Casa, sent a copy of the 1549 *Catalogo* to Rome, reporting that 'one of the principal men' of the Venetian senate opposed it because it 'listed a work composed by a friend'. Grendler thinks the work was probably *Espositione letterale del testo di Matteo Evangelista* by Bernardino

57

Tomitano, a popular Paduan professor of logic enjoying favour in Venice. In 1547, Tomitano published (as his own work) Erasmus's paraphrase of Matthew's Gospel (the above title), and both the 1549 *Catalogo* and the 1554 Index accepted his authorship and banned the work. According to Grendler: 'While the bookmen were criticizing the new Index, Tomitano spontaneously appeared before the Venetian Holy Office to exculpate himself. He testified that he had translated the work for a third party, who had borne the publication costs and that the Venetian inquisitor (Fra Marino) had approved it with minor corrections.'[119] In his appearance of 9 August, Marino contradicted Tomitano and claimed he had refused to approve the work but had been ignored by both the author and the secretary of Riformatori dello Studio (at Tomitano's university, Padua). Tomitano had the book stamped without licence. When Marino protested, the secretary 'simply shrugged his shoulders'.

Marino further states that Tomitano's book 'was brought to him by a young man for him to have a look at' and that his first reaction was that 'he did not like the style'. Marino appears to be caught in the middle of a number of forces in his defence. After its reorganisation in 1547 – five years into Marino's term of office – the Inquisition in Venice began to confiscate and burn books, but it was neither more severe nor more lenient there than in any of the other Italian cities. There was in Venice, however, an important difference in attitude towards other faiths: that city, due to its strategic location and enterprise at commerce was fairly tolerant towards the heterodox foreigners in its midst – German Lutherans in particular. Venetians had more opportunity then most Italians for contact with men of different religious views, yet this tolerance did not extend to allowing a significant portion of the population to embrace heresy, and during Marino's time there was a certain alarm over Lutheran influence from the north. The Venetian state and Church wished to handle matters with a minimum of pressure from Rome, and many Venetians thought of their Church almost as a department of the republic.

With the spirit of the Counter-Reformation behind him, Paul III urged the Venetians to consider stronger action against heretics and their books. Members of his court became increasingly pointed in their criticism of Venetian tolerance. In the 1540s the republic tried to steer a middle course over the conflict between the Emperor Charles V and the German Lutheran princes. While Marino was inquisitor, the papal nuncio, Della Casa, reported to the pope that the Venetians were ready to take stricter control regarding the heretics in their midst. There is more than a strong hint that Rome felt the administration of the Inquisition to be a bit lax. The preaching of heresy by an Augustinian friar in the Church of St. Barnabas(!) in Venice caused alarm, and the evidence suggests that light punishment and commutation marked the Inquisition before the arrival of Fra Peretti. Trials in 1548 and 1549 saw that books were burned and owners were fined; but rarely was investigation made of the accused, and frequently they did not even appear in court.

In the Holy Office documents Marino states that he is chaplain to Piero Loredano; and though we know nothing of Piero as an individual, the Loredano family was clearly an influential one in Venetian history – there were three Loredano doges. Interestingly, one of the Loredano palaces is only a short distance from the above-mentioned Church of St. Barnabas. The position of father inquisitor was a prestigious one, and Grendler notes that it was often a stepping-stone to preferment in the Venetian Church: a number of inquisitors were later elevated to the episcopate.[120] Except for the mention of his being Piero Loredano's chaplain, we know nothing of Marino's career following his time as inquisitor. The Holy Office papers may indicate why: he emotionally accuses a number of individuals of conspiring against him.

In one of his appearances before the court he asks that a certain person be excluded from giving judgement on him: 'I, Master Marino the Venetian reject Nicolò the Inquisitor, as a suspect person in my case as he is my bitter enemy, who for many years now with some accomplices of his has always plotted against me, and has continuously slandered me.' In another statement he says that Nicolò 'has been notorious in all my convent for many years now'. From other files in the Venetian archives we know that Nicolò, a Venetian Franciscan, was Marino's successor and held the office of father inquisitor until 1557, when Peretti came to Venice. Peretti was succeeded by the Dominican, Fra Tommaso, from Vicenza. In Marino's 1555 'list of enemies' there is the name of one cleric, Tommaso, who may be the same individual.

Two names appear in the 1561 proceeding whose careers are well known: Annibale Grisonio and Pier Paolo Vergerio. The last documented appearance of Marino – oddly, six years after the 1555 trials – is mainly concerned with Vergerio, the famous Bishop of Capodistria who became a Protestant minister and an influential protagonist. Like many other suspect Venetian clerics, Marino was apparently charged with being either influenced by Vergerio or too

59

lenient regarding his writings. Marino protests in 1561: 'Vergerio has falsified for many years now the gospel ... and profaned the ... sacred writings (gospels) themselves'. What follows that remark is particularly difficult to translate, but Gavin Ryan has suggested: 'and could have faked something written by me having been composed by him' or 'I could have made some writing (or letter)... having been composed by him.'

At the same session, Monsignor Annibale Grisonio, inquisitor commissary, gave evidence against Marino:

> 'I tell the truth about which I know to be the truth ... The truth found ... many responsible came out of Capodistria (Vergerio's see), and appeared (before me) and in such manoeuvering I linked one of these young people to the said Marino inquisitor ... I saw that the said Marino was familiar with these writings of Capodistria (apparently Vergerio's).' Grisonio goes on to say that 'being there a party in the house of Fra Marino with an acquaintance of mine ... it was impossible to reason with the said Fra Marino this friend of mine ... told me Marino had used different words. I cannot remember precisely, but to be quite honest I was scandalized to hear such words coming out of the mouth of an inquisitor.'[121]

It is difficult to get the full impact of what Grisonio was charging, but in other documents from the file it is clear that we are dealing with the realm of rumours: rumours of Marino 'showing favours', being 'involved with suspect persons', being 'given to luxury' – and, most oddly, 'profaning sacred objects'. There is little doubt that, like Peretti, Marino had his share of enemies – an occupational hazard! But it goes further: Marino feels he is the victim of many 'plots' against him. As before, Marino in the 1561 appearance is highly defensive about his performance as inquisitor and proclaims, 'I will always be a fierce enemy of the Lutherans.'

The links with Grisonio and Vergerio are interesting, and possibly help us fill in some of the gaps. A native of Vergerio's home town and see city, Capodistria, called Annibale Grisonio, was attached to the household of Giovanni Della Casa, papal nuncio 1544-9, and aided both him and Marino with the trial and negotiations concerning Vergerio. So successful was Grisonio that the Venetian government authorised his going to Capodistria to assist the local inquisitor, and afterwards to Pirano and Pola on the Dalmatian coast. According to Grendler,

Grisonio's zeal sometimes exceeded his judgment. In 1551, (the new nuncio) (Beccadelli) heard a rumour that Rome had sent Grisonio a list of 200 Venetian noblemen, including leading members of the government, accused of being Protestants. The horror-struck nuncio frantically inquired, and Rome assured him that, although the names of many nobles had appeared in inquisition trials, no list had been sent to anyone. The nuncio's fears were little eased. Because of the 'immoderate zeal' and 'little judgement' of Grisonio and others, he warned, the papacy ran a grave risk of provoking the Venetians 'to hate the pope'.[122]

Grendler notes that, interestingly, Grisonio was partly independent of the nuncio and maintained his own communication with Rome.

Giovanni Della Casa, who was nuncio for most of Marino's career as inquisitor, is well known in history for his dissipated youth and his work on courtly etiquette, *Galateo*. The three major figures of the Venetian Inquisition were the father inquisitor, the nuncio, and the patriarch: they alone had decisive votes. Marino could not have dealt with a more exotic ecclesiastic than Della Casa. Born into a wealthy landowning family near Florence, he studied law and took minor orders in Rome, apparently with no intention of proceeding to the priesthood. Having secured employment in the papal government, in 1544 he was elected Archbishop of Benevento. He was ordained priest in order to qualify for the office – and never visited his diocese. In the same year he was appointed nuncio to Venice. As the pope's representative, his duties were to ward off the influence of Charles V on Venice and to repress any nascent Protestantism. He indicted Vergerio for heresy, and in 1549 the pope announced in consistory the deposition of the Bishop of Capodistria. It is argued that Vergerio's scathing denunciation of Della Casa on moral grounds may have impeded his ecclesiastical advancement: the latter's nunciature ended with the death of Paul III, and though he later became secretary of state under Paul IV he was never made a cardinal.

Pier Paolo Vergerio is a fascinating individual and in many respects a likely candidate for writing something like *The Gospel of Barnabas* were it not for the fact that he died twenty years before Sixtus V was made pope. Vergerio's early career is similar to that of Della Casa: he came from a family of substance in Capodistria and studied law at Padua, becoming a judge and a lawyer. In 1527 he joined the service of the Church as a layman, and six years later was made papal nuncio to Germany. Vergerio was involved in Rome's attempts to achieve a negotiated settlement with the Lutherans. He seemed to be the very man for the situation because of his open mind; unlike many others, he was accurately acquainted with the spread of Lutheranism. Vergerio warned Paul III of the true state of affairs, complaining that the pontiff naïvely saw Hungary as more important than Germany. He met Luther and was impressed by him, remarking 'although 50 years of age, he was strong and hearty and looked not yet 40.' In 1536, he was made bishop, first of a diocese in Crotia and then of his native city.[123]

In 1544 Vergerio was accused of holding Lutheran ideas, and in 1549 he went into exile, first in Switzerland and then in Wurtemberg, where he was counsellor to the duke. This post he held until his death in 1565. It is said that he became convinced it was God's will he should become a Protestant at the deathbed of Francesco Spiera, an Italian Lutheran who had retracted his conversion. In exile Vergerio wrote prolifically in defence of Protestantism; and as Von Pastor views it, 'the keen wit and glowing hate of an apostate were now devoted to the warfare against the papacy'.[124]

Before Horatio Brown's discovery of the 1549 *Catalogo* in the Biblioteca Marciana, our knowledge of that Index had depended on the hostile edition Vergerio had published in 1549. Vergerio reviled what he termed 'Della Casa's Index' for its many errors and careless compilation. He charged that Della Casa had to call to his aid 'certain monks' (like Marino) apparently scarcely better equipped than himself for such a production. He complained that in the Index there were no obscene publications, such as Della Casa's own *Capitolo del Forno*. Vergerio's personal denunciation of Della Casa had pointed to the hypocrisy of one responsible for a list of prohibited books being the author of obscene verse. Vergerio ridiculed the entire procedure of the Inquisition and the Index in a series of pamphlets modelled on the satirist Pietro Aretino's open letter addressed to princes and other influential persons. His satirical 1554 *Letter of the Three Bishops* professed to be a letter of advice given by three bishops to the pope to help strengthen the power of the papacy and was widely used as a polemical tool by Protestants. Vergerio's name became anathema in Catholic circles, and a number of influential Venetian bookmen and ecclesiastics were linked to his influence in the 1550s and 1560s. One publisher, Arrivabene, was accused in 1549 of sharing Vergerio's heretical views; interestingly, it was he who in 1547 published the first Italian translation of the Koran.

A case can be made for Fra Marino, father inquisitor of Venice from 1542 to 50, being the likely author of *Barnabas*. If we assume, as the preface to the Spanish translation seems to assert, that Italian was the original language of *Barnabas* and that a 'Fra Marino' of the time of Sixtus V was involved in its discovery, many other pieces begin to fall into place. I find it easier to accept the Raggs' opinion of 1907 than subsequent theories put forward by other scholars. There are, however, a few obstacles in maintaining this original assessment, and there is one other possibility concerning the authorship of *Barnabas* which must be presented.

Jan Slomp explores a case for 'Fra Marino' being one of the Marranos who came from Iberia to Italy.[125] The term *Marrano* ('pig') was one of derision for Jewish converts (*Conversos*) in Spain and Portugal. Jewish life in Christian Iberia flourished until the fourteenth century. Then the Jews came under increasing pressure followed by the great persecutions of 1391. Some Jews were killed, others fled, and there were large-scale conversions, creating a sizeable community of 'New Christians,' as they were called. In the fifteenth century the Conversos were more and more regarded with suspicion by the 'Old Christians': they were heretics, as it was said that outwardly most of them adhered to the forms of Catholicism but secretly continued to practise Judaism. Most of them had been poorly instructed in their new faith, and in time the old and prosperous Marrano families were seen as a threat. In 1492 their Catholic Majesties Ferdinand and Isabella celebrated the surrender of Muslim Granada and signed a decree expelling all Jews from Spain. Many Marranos migrated to Holland, Turkey and Italy.

Slomp suggests that 'Marino' may have been the chosen Italian name for a formerly Jewish Fra Marino because it reminded him of the nickname forced on his people. He might have been a Converso in the school of the Franciscan monastery overseen by Fra Peretti – maybe even a novice. Apparently the persecution of the Conversos who had come to Venice for refuge reached its height during Peretti's regime.

The major impetus for considering a Spanish link for the authorship of *Barnabas* has come from the studies of the Spanish scholar Mikel de Epalza, who has sought to identify the author among Christian converts to Islam. A central problem with the Vienna manuscript has been its extraordinary linguistic incongruities: Venetian and Tuscan elements in the Italian; the poorly rendered Arabic notes; Latin spellings clearly indicating the influence of the Vulgate Bible; and a general Renaissance orthography, plus influences from the writings of Dante. As Slomp has said: 'There is no other manuscript extant with such a strange combination of linguistic elements as far as morphology, syntax, strand of dialects etc. are concerned.' One peculiarity for which no satisfactory answer has been given is why there are so many 'h's in the text which do not belong in proper Italian; 'Hanno' for *anno* ('year') is one example. There are many inconsistencies in spelling. Slomp notes that in Chapters 3 and 4 of *Barnabas* we have '*immenso splendore*', '*imenso splendore*' and '*inmenso splendore*'. In his opinion, 'This is proof of the author's failure to master the language he was using.'[126]

Part of this linguistic complication might be understandable if the author had been a Spanish student in a university like Bologna, where both the Tuscan and Venetian dialects were spoken. According to de Epalza, it was quite common for Spaniards to be studying there. The language of the university was, of course, Latin, but Fra Marino would have learned his Italian from what he heard in conversation. As Slomp says, de Epalza's 'suggestion is not merely hypothetical because we know about at least one student from Majorca, Anselmo Turmeda, who studied in Bologna for ten years. According to his biography, he became a Muslim' (1383-90).[127] Despite the obvious difficulty with time, Anselmo Turmeda is an interesting possibility for 'Fra Marino'; apparently, he claimed to have been a priest before his conversion to Islam and said his teacher in Bologna was a 'Crypto-Muslim'. De Epalza wrote about him in 1972, and says he was a converted Franciscan who took revenge on Christianity after his conversion to Islam.[128]

Slomp studied the writings of Anselmo Turmeda (who became Abd-Allah ibn Abd Allah) and was 'convinced ... of the fact that he cannot be the author of Pseudo-Barnabas'. Turmeda derived most of his arguments against Christianity from the Spanish Muslim writer Ibn Hazm of Cordoba (994-1064); like the author of *Barnabas*, he has no real knowledge of Greek. There are other reasons for a Spanish connection. There are a number of contemporary gospel forgeries in Arabic which were discovered in Granada after 1588, and the forgers were two *Moriscos* (Moors). Coins mentioned in Chapter 54 of the Italian manuscript – golden *denarius* divided into sixty *minuti* – have been identified as Spanish. There is also the fact that George Sale said, 'Of this Gospel the Moriscos in Africa have a translation in Spanish.' De Epalza points to a reference to this Spanish text in Tunis dated 1643.[129]

The preface to the Spanish text containing the Fra Marino story says that a Spanish Muslim, Mostafa de Aranda, translated the Italian text into Spanish.[130] As his name indicates, Mostafa came from Aranda, where Philip II deported and settled the remaining Moriscos of Granada hoping to achieve assimilation into the local population. Slomp thinks it possible that Fra Marino and Mostafa were the same person – converts often changed their names[131]. Having Fra Marino as a Spaniard by birth, later to be converted to Islam, would help explain why the author's knowledge of the Koran was so incomplete. Perhaps he used a Jewish traveller from Turkey for the Arabic marginal notes; several Jewish refugees had gone to Istanbul.

Presenting Fra Marino as a Spanish Converso answers a few of the complexities of the authorship question, but in my opinion also unnecessarily interjects many others. Basically, it removes us from the known facts as given in the Fra Marino/Sixtus V account, and there is considerable evidence that we are dealing with an *Italian* author. The atmosphere of late medieval Italy pervades much of the gospel, as has been noted. The Christian spirituality of the late Middle Ages is well known to him, and there is a monkish, devotional element to many of the chapters of *Barnabas*. The author is also well versed in Dante and scholastic theology.

The preface to the Spanish text referred to by George Sale which unexpectedly 'resurfaced' in Australia in 1976, was presented by J. F. Fletcher.[132] I did not see it until after my research in Venice, and the information it gives seems to confirm my general hypothesis concerning authorship – as well as increasing the mystery regarding the curious figure of Fra Marino. Readers acquainted with Sale's account of the Spanish preface will be fascinated by what he did not relate concerning the Fra Marino 'story' – and by what to me looks like confirmation that the Fra Marino of the preface was the father inquisitor Marino of Venice.[133] The preface (which appears to be the words of Fra Marino) states that he was 'in the office of defining papal cases and had a hand in the inquisition' (*estando en el officio de la difinicion de los casos Papales, y teniendo mano en la inquisicion*).

The preface reads like an apologia. The title indicates that it is a prologue *to the reader* from Fra Marino, and we have what Fletcher terms 'the gentle warning', *del que por mal nombre se llamo Fray Marin*, which could be translated as something like 'one with the bad reputation' or 'for want of a better name'. This certainly fits the known facts of the inquisitor Fra Marino. In the introduction, Marino says he has pondered for some time the matter of the

65

interpretation of scripture and the development of the biblical canon; even the educated have difficulty understanding scripture. Many thoughts have 'run through his mind': in all the calamities the Jews suffered over the centuries, surely some of their holy books were lost?

While still inquisitor, Marino was visited by a gentleman of the house of Ursina (Orsina or Orsini?) who brought him four ancient books written in Latin which he thought were probably heretical. They were given to Fra Marino to dispose of. The gentleman said the books were from his family library. When Marino had free time he read the four, discovering them to be new commentaries(?) or versions of Isaiah, Ezekiel, Daniel and Joel.

This experience caused Marino to do some more thinking: 'I thought it impossible that only four gospels were written when there were twelve apostles. Surely more existed.' Then he remembered the disagreement that had existed between Paul and Barnabas, and was further convinced it was impossible there were only four Gospels. We are gradually being led to the real point of the preface: the 'discovery' of *The Gospel of Barnabas*. For about a year Marino thought along these lines, and then he had another visitor: this time the widow of a member of the Colona (Colonna?) family came across three books in the inventory of her husband's effects. Her son had read one which spoke badly of St. Paul, and she decided to bring them to Fra Marino in secret. She pleaded that he should not mention where they came from for fear that her husband's body would be taken from its grave and burned. Marino agreed to her wishes and later looked at the books.

One was about the Virgin; another was by Zizimo, a 'disciple of the apostles'; and the last by Irenaeus. The last-named used as its source of anti-Pauline attack *The Gospel of Barnabas*, of which Marino said, 'Think now, brother, the longing I had to find this gospel.' The Fra Marino/Sixtus V story of the discovery of the gospel in the papal library follows, and the only element which Sale did not stress is the statement that the two were 'many times alone dealing with business in secret'. God made him a friend of Sixtus, and Marino charges the reader to profit by reading the gospel he has discovered and give God thanks for what he receives from it. He says he studied the gospel for two years and then decided to *venir a la fee* ('come to the faith', that is to say the Muslim faith).

Page 5 of the introduction bears the heading 'In the name of Allah' and states the well-known information that Mostafa de Aranda translated *The Gospel of Barnabas* from Italian into

Castilian. Fletcher ends his article by saying that he had tried unsuccessfully to check out the proper names and references using 'the resources of the largest library in the Southern Hemisphere [the Fisher]' but found a 'skilful camouflage and smoke-screen'. The name Ursina could possibly be Orsina or Orsini, well-known Italian family names; alternatively it could be a disguise: *ursinus* is Latin for 'bear'. The Colonna family is, of course, one of the most illustrious in Roman history. I have found records of at least two well-known Colonnas in sixteenth-century Venice: the Dominican friar Francesco Colonna of SS. John and Paul and the sculptor Iacopo Colonna who died in 1540.

Jan Slomp remarks: 'It is *theoretically* possible that more than one person was involved in the fabrication of this gospel. This *may* explain the contradictions, because one person trusted the other's expertise and did not double check it.'[134] To a certain extent I think this line of approach is worth exploring. A 'scenario' of sorts concerning the authorship of *Barnabas* can be presented, and in the following I have mixed the known historical data with some conjecture based on those facts.

Fra Marino, a Franciscan monk known for his preaching ability and organisational skills (both can be seen from the compilation of *Barnabas*), became the father inquisitor of Venice in 1542. Initially he performed his office in a manner that was perfectly acceptable: neither too lenient nor too stern for Venetian tastes. In 1547, after the arrival of Giovanni Della Casa, the Venetian Inquisition was reorganised and began to confiscate and burn books; a good impression was thus given to Rome that something was being done in Venice. In 1549 a *Catalogo di diverse opere* was drawn up under the leadership of Marino and Della Casa, but it was never fully implemented in Venice. Annibale Grisonio with his special connections with Rome and close relationship with Della Casa, must have been an irritation to Marino. He received much of the credit for handling the Vergerio affair and was sent to neighbouring towns in the republic to aid the local inquisitors.

Two years before Peretti arrived as inquisitor, an inquiry was held by the Holy Office which included queries regarding Marino's administration. Marino was charged with leniency, especially regarding suspects influenced by Lutheranism. A number of other charges were also aired: he had shown favours while in office, and had made statements which for a father inquisitor were highly questionable. Peretti's appointment by his old friend was to be a house-cleaning – both of the Inquisition and the Franciscan order.

The 'foreigner' was despised both as inquisitor and rector of the Venetian Franciscans. We can speculate that the new inquisitor viewed the composer of the 1549 *Catalogo* as ineffectual and in no small part responsible for the laxity of the Venetian Inquisition: Marino had held office for eight years. Della Casa was now dead, and his responsibility would have been forgotten; besides, he had had the favour of Paul IV. It is possible that Marino was in the very convent where Peretti resided as director of studies. We know nothing of the former until his appearance before the Holy Office in 1561, when he stated he was chaplain to Piero Loredano. That position could easily have been filled by a member of the convent. Baron Hubner writes that as rector of the Franciscans, Peretti's 'special mission was to reform the convents, to introduce into them a strict observance of the rules, and therefore to fight against the useless and the lukewarm'.[135]

There are any number of reasons why Marino grew to despise Peretti, and an obvious one was jealousy. Despite his ultimate recall from Venice, Peretti went on to preferment after preferment, becoming procurator-general and vicar-general of the Franciscans, Bishop of Sant'Agata dei Goti, cardinal and, finally pope. Fra Marino went nowhere as far as we know. Almost every analyst of *Barnabas* has noted the motive of revenge against Sixtus V in the writing of the gospel. There are many portions of the work which can be read as slaps at the hierarchy. The author speaks of 'True Pharisees' in opposition to the false ones which read like assaults on his contemporaries. The author's attack on St. Paul and those who would make Jesus God contains an undertone of hostility towards the Catholic establishment.

In the Spanish preface the point is made that 'God of his mercy' had made Fra Marino 'very intimate with Pope Sixtus V'. It seems unlikely – but not impossible – that Sixtus mellowed toward the now ageing monk and received him at the Vatican. The preface to the Sydney manuscript has Marino claiming he and the pope were involved in *secret business*. It is difficult to know just what the relationship was. We are somewhat reminded of another pope, Leo X, and his favourite buffoon, Fra Mariano, who used to hold poetic contests: Latin verses were batted from one to the other as in a tennis match, and the loser was forced to drink down at once a full beaker of wine.

It is possible that the link with Sixtus V was no more than a device employed by the author. There is the point of hypocrisy which might have some play here. As with the scandal of Della Casa (the writer of obscene verse, in Vergerio's eyes) the hypocrisy of Peretti, a former inquisitor, possessing examples of the very books Marino should have been more zealous in destroying may have been known to him. One does not have to stretch the scenario far to envision an old monk (Marino would probably have been about seventy when Sixtus was crowned) embittered over many years; the wounds of Grisonio, Della Casa and a number of others from those days when he was inquisitor; the indignity of being associated with Vergerio. The introduction to the Sydney manuscript indicates – falsely or not – a questioning monk, one who asks if there is any value in scriptural books not included in the church's canon. There seems to be (at least a hint of) genuine curiosity here. One also wonders whether Marino – like so many other clerics – was chagrined at Peretti's ineptitude in the revision of St. Jerome's Bible. Who knows where his true sympathies may have been? There is also the matter of the odd confidence which seems to be given the inquisitor by the Ursina gentleman and *'una dama de la casa Colona'*; obviously, they would not have approached Marino if they expected him to turn them in. The veil of mystery is lifted a little here – but unfortunately, not far enough.

The last element of the Spanish preface's story – 'that by the reading of which [*The Gospel of Barnabas*] he became a convert to Mohammedanism' – brings us to the most difficult element of this reconstruction. The former father inquisitor Fra Marino as a bona fide convert to Islam: why are there no clues to this? Was it an incredibly hushed-up matter? Did it really occur? There were at that time a number of well-known Italian apostate clergy, like Vergerio, Bernardino Ochino, the brilliant preacher and vicar-general of the Capuchin order, and the Augustinian prior Pietro Vermigli, but they went over to Protestantism. The author of *Barnabas*, be he the inquisitor Fra Marino or not, seems to have made no public attempt to make himself known as a Muslim convert.

The author's lack of acquaintance with the Koran is another factor worth considering. Father Jomier has commented that the author of *Barnabas* does not rely on the letter of the Koran, contrary to the manner in which he employs New Testament material: 'He is a forger, and would betray himself too quickly if he gave textual references. He is, however, inspired by the Koran – there are more than thirty allusions to its text.'[136] According to Jomier, he uses Muslim sources not as books but as ideas, images. The writer speaks of Islam as one who has learned about it from conversation. He also

69

seems to have been exposed to commentaries on the koranic text – or at least, to popular traditions and developments of what the Koran presents. Nowhere is this more evident than with the account of Judas' substitution. It seems likely that the author read or was told an account like that given by Wahb (see page 45), which by the sixteenth century had become a popular explanation of the koranic denial of Jesus' death on the cross.

There would have been many opportunities for the Fra Marino of the Holy Office documents to have learned of Islam: the father inquisitor was expected to be well versed in the faiths of the heretic and the infidel. I think it feasible that Fra Marino may have become acquainted with Islam through the Marranos in Venice and that following his difficulties with the Holy Office he perhaps became fascinated by that religion. The 1561 appearance before the Holy Office was in many ways a final blow; and possibly, because Islam was considered to be an ultimate rejection of the Christian establishment, he chose it as the vehicle through which to vent his revenge against Peretti and those like him. The Sydney manuscript preface states that Marino pondered the matter for two years after the 'discovery' of *The Gospel of Barnabas*.

There could be any number of variations on this theme. It can also be conjectured that Marino used a Marrano scribe to write his vindictive gospel and, as Slomp suggests, accepted the Muslim expertise of his 'co-author' along with his competence in writing Italian. I had several handwriting experts compare what in Busta 12 appears to be the handwritten statement of Fra Marino the inquisitor with the writing of the Vienna manuscript, and they suggested that both *could* have come from the same individual. There is the possibility that Marino taught his scribe how to write a convincing manuscript and that the latter aped his master's writing. We also have to consider Marino's probable age at the time of Sixtus V's pontificate.

Perhaps Fra Marino never lived to see the completed work, and the subsequent Spanish translation (which, according to one source, ended up among the Moriscos in Africa) presented the story of its 'composition' as a kind of explanatory note. I think we would have to consider matters differently if the reverse were the case and the Vienna manuscript had the Fra Marino story, whereas the Spanish version did not. Fra Marino's scribe/ friend/co-author could have also been responsible for the Turkish binding and Arabic notes. Fra Marino was therefore the spokesman of *Barnabas*, and its Spanish and other peculiarities are due in large part to the inscriber.

Fra Marino consciously aimed at a singular gospel notion, as with the Diatessaron and the koranic idea of 'gospel'. He developed a colourful narrative of the rejection of the doctrinal foundation of Christianity: the Passion, death and Resurrection of Jesus. He betrayed his background as a Christian preacher in proclaiming the new 'true gospel' and 'true prophet'. It is conceivable that he discovered an apocryphal *Gospel of Barnabas* and used it as the basis of his work; if not, what better choice of name for a lost gospel than that of 'Barnabas', already the title of a lost gospel to be found in the Pseudo-Gelasian decree?

It is possible that Fra Marino was never converted to Islam and used the religion as a vehicle for taking revenge. He may have had pieces like Vergerio's *Letter to Three Bishops* in mind. The Venice of his age knew many examples of imitating manuscripts and ancient writers; Norman Cohn describes several forgeries regarding the Inquisition and the *Pseudo-Batolean Consilia* published in Venice in 1590.[137] The writings of Angelo Beolco, nicknamed 'Il Ruzzante', (1502-42) revealed anticlericalism and a mistrust of the papacy. There are any number of possibilities, and we may never know the full story of the conception of *Barnabas* unless other evidence comes to light, but the author does seem to disclose his identity both in the Spanish preface and, as we have seen, on two occasions in the gospel itself.

It is likely the 'Jubilee Year' passage pinpoints the date of *Barnabas* as the year of Peretti's being crowned pope – for Marino, the ultimate perturbation. The finding of the 'hidden true book of Moses' by Nicodemus in the temple also gives him away (see pages 43-4). As Slomp has pointed out, the implication of this passage is 'that the true gospel of Barnabas will only be discovered at the ... time ... of its author, that is 1585 at the Jubilee instituted by Pope Sixtus V'[138]

The irony is, of course, that *Barnabas* did not surface until the eighteenth century, and in Amsterdam; and that it should have been two Anglicans named Ragg who at the beginning of this century made the work well known in the world of the 'true prophet'. I can imagine that following the death of Fra Marino his new 'friends' among the Marranos were not quite certain what to make of this creation now that the inspiration behind it had gone. More likely it was just forgotten in time and passed through several hands in Venice as some sort of curio, later to come into the possession of the aspostate Gregorio Leti, the most listed writer ever on the Index of Prohibited Books and a biographer of Marino's old antagonist, Sixtus V. In an odd sense, *Barnabas* had come full circle.

Postscript to Chapter 4

Following the completion of this manuscript, I received permission to go through the archives of the Order of Friars Minor Conventual in Rome, and found information which was not available in Venice. There were a number of items about the one-time father inquisitor of Venice, Fra Marino. Most importantly there was a surname – Moro. Fra Marino Moro was from one of the most important noble families of the republic, and one ancestor, Cristoforo Moro, Doge from 1462-71, has been suggested as the 'original' Othello of Shakespeare's play. The origin of this highly appropriate name for the author of the Muslim *Gospel of Barnabas* is not known, but *moro* has been a common Italian and Spanish designation for Muslim. The Venetians used the word to describe the inhabitants of the Muslim Maghreb, and the famed Saracen pirate who preyed on Venetian ships in the Adriatic in the 1530s was called 'Il Moro of Alexandria'.

An alternative suggestion has been that the name originated from the Morea, the medieval Peloponnesus, and this has appealed to those who feel Othello was not a Moor but a Venetian gentleman named Moro. The name survives in Italy: Aldo Moro the premier who was murdered.

Fra Marino Moro was far more important in the Order of Friars Minor Conventual than materials kept in Venice indicate. The date of his birth is not known, but he died 8 November 1597 at the celebrated convent of Santa Maria Gloriosa de Frari in Venice, probably at the age of eighty. Marino Moro entered the order as a youth at the Frari, and was greatly influenced by the friar and theologian to the Council of Trent, Cornelio Musso (1511-74). Musso was a renowned preacher and called 'the Demosthenes of Italy' by his contemporaries. In 1575, Moro was responsible for collecting his mentor's sermons for publication.

The year before Marino Moro became inquisitor of Venice he was elected guardian of the Frari, a position later held by the future Pope Sixtus V. Two years before Moro's last appearance before the Holy Office in Venice (1561), he went to Rome as secretary-general of his order. Moro remained in Rome in this office until 1566, and

1 Facsimile of pages 1 and 734 of the Vienna manuscript of the Gospel of Barnabas. The heading for page one reads: 'True Gospel of Jesus, called Christ, a new prophet sent by God to the world: according to the description of Barnabas his apostle'. Österreichische Nationalbibliothek, Vienna.

2 The Prunksaal (Grand Hall) of the Austrian National Library at Vienna containing the famous collection of Prince Eugene of Savoy. *Osterreichische National-bibliothek, Vienna.*

3 Barnabas and Paul in the cartoon by Raphael, *The Sacrifice at Lystra*, in the Victoria and Albert Museum, London. Property of HM The Queen. *The Victoria and Albert Museum.*

4 St Paul by Rembrandt. *Kunsthistorisches Museum, Vienna.*

5   Portrait of Sixtus V, showing achievements of his pontificate including the Vatican Library. *British Museum.*

CATALOGO

DI DIVERSE OPERE,

COMPOSITIONI, ET LIBRI;

li quali come heretici, sospetti, impij, & scandalosi si dichiarano dannati, & prohibiti in questa inclita citta di Vinegia, & in tutto l'Illustrissimo domino Vinitiano, si da mare, come da terra:

Composto dal Reuerendo padre maestro MARINO Vinitiano, del monastero de frati Minori di Vinegia, dell'ordine di San Francesco, de conuentuali, Inquisitore dell'heretica prauita; con maturo cosiglio, essaminatione, & comprobatione di molti Reuerendi Primarij maestri in Theologia di diuerse religioni, & monasteri di detta citta di Vinegia: d'ordine, & comissione del Reuerendissimo Monsignor GIOVANNI DELLA CASA, eletto di Beneuento, Decano della camera Apostolica di sua SANTITA, & della Santa sede Apostolica in tutto l'Illustriss. Dominio predetto Legato Apostolico: aggiutoui anchora il consiglio de i clarissimi Signori Deputati contra gli heretici: stampato in essecutione della parte presa nell'eccellentissimo Consiglio de Dieci con la giunta; à laude del Signore IDDIO, conseruation della fede Christiana, & felicita di esso Illustrissimo Dominio.

In Vinegia, alla bottega d'Erasmo di Vincenzo Valgrisi.
M. D. XLIX.

6 Title page of the original printing of the 1549 *Catalogo di diverse opere . . .* (the catalogue of prohibited books executed during Fra Marino's term as father inquisitor). *Biblioteca Nazionale Marciana, Venice.*

was also given the purely honorary position of provincial minister of the Holy Land. In 1566 Moro returned to Venice, and a year later Fra Peretti (the future Sixtus V who was then vicar apostolic of the order) made him Commissario Generale for the Frari.

From 1574 to 1578, Moro was provincial minister of the Venetian province of Saint Anthony. Interestingly there is no particular post listed for him from 1578 to 1592. Sixtus V's pontificate was from 1585 to 1590; and when Gregory XIII became pope in 1572 Peretti had fallen into disfavour and retired to a villa on the slopes of the Esquiline. Two years after Sixtus V's death, Marino Moro was again Commissario Generale of the Frari, and reconfirmed in that post until the year before he died.

The reader is faced with a great amount of speculation over the authorship of *Barnabas* in Chapter 4 and this new information intensifies the possibilities. Marino Moro's position in his religious order, the fact that he appeared at one time to have had the favour of Fra Peretti, and his career in Rome – all this has to be taken into consideration. Marino Moro was able to survive the Holy Office inquests of 1555 and 1561, and go on to advancement in his order, but there is the curious period of fourteen years when he occupied no particular position. Significantly, this occurs during Sixtus V's pontificate. There is the heightened possibility that the name 'Fra Marino' was chosen by the author of *Barnabas* for its obvious symbolism. What better choice of 'author' than a father inquisitor whose surname was *Moro*? Like Sixtus V, perhaps Marino Moro was the object of a literary act of revenge. Was the author a monk who equally despised Peretti and Moro? A victim of their administrations of the inquisition in Venice? It is a pity the Venetian and Roman archives preserve only the cold, bare facts. One suspects the full story has disappeared – or has been destroyed.

PART TWO

'The Gospel according to the Muslims'

CHAPTER FIVE

'Allah's Uncreated Speech': How Christians and Muslims differ in their Interpretation of Scripture

It is an irony that a sixteenth-century gospel which seems likely to have been composed by a former Venetian father inquisitor in revenge against his successor is still actively utilised by various Muslim polemicists. It is also ironic that the dissection of that document has been achieved by the use of critical methods Muslims are not allowed in approaching their scriptures. An analysis of *Barnabas* opens up a more important issue of how Muslims and Christians differ in their interpretation of their respective holy books. We have seen how the author of *Barnabas* frequently acts as an interpreter of and commentator on koranic truth. On several occasions he makes clear what the Koran merely implies: he elaborates the direction in which several koranic passages seem to point. The result in several instances sets *The Gospel of Barnabas* at variance with the Koran. Any discussion of the polemical use of this gospel has to come to terms with what is probably the greatest divide between Christians and Muslims: the issue of critical analysis of the scriptures.

The Muslim attitude towards the Koran is usually described as 'fundamentalist', a word which has re-entered the popular vocabulary along with all sorts of new implications and emotions. The term, like so many others applied to Islam by Westerners, has a history steeped in Christians' coming to terms with their Bible in the last two centuries. With rare exceptions, there was no interpretation of scripture other than a 'fundamentalist' one prior to the middle of the nineteenth century – certainly to the man in the pew. The word 'fundamentalist' originated at a series of late nineteenth-century Bible conferences in the United States, where a strict view of biblical inerrancy and literalistic interpretation of the Bible was upheld. 'Five Points' (fundamentals) of truth were issued: the plenary inspiration and inerrancy of scripture; the deity of Jesus; his virgin birth and substitutionary blood atonement; his bodily Resurrection; and pre-millennial second coming. A series of books entitled *The Fundamentals*,[139] endowed by the Los Angeles Bible Institute, was widely circulated in 1909, and the word 'fundamentalist' came to be the rallying epithet of those opposed to the 'Modernism' preached in the pulpits and theological seminaries of the main-line denominations.

'Dangerous elements' were entering the American religious scene with the advent from Germany of the critical study of the Bible: what came to be called 'higher criticism'. This approach emanated largely from the application of new concepts of German philosophy to explain the structure of the Bible. Higher criticism investigated the literary methods used by the authors of the books of the Old and New Testament. This was to be distinguished from 'lower criticism', which was concerned with finding the oldest – and presumably the most reliable – manuscripts and the best translations of them. Higher criticism viewed the texts of the Bible in the same manner as it would other written texts: namely as the work of human minds with various sources, layers and interpolations.

One result of this procedure is well known to me from my days (1958–61) at Union Theological Seminary in New York. The first important project for new seminarians at that time was what we affectionately termed the 'Pentateuch paper', a lengthy analysis of passages from Genesis in the light of the 'documentary theory' as promulgated by the German scholar Julius Wellhausen. The Graf-Wellhausen school of Old Testament criticism dissected the first five books of the Bible into different strata. The 'five books of Moses' were an interweaving of four major sources: the Yahwist and Elohist (termed by the different Hebrew names for God, Yahweh and Elohim); and the Priestly and Deuteronomic. I remember marking a bible with four colourations for the various strata – it seemed very convincing proof of the theory at the time! The New Testament was the next challenge, and at the beginning of the twentieth century scholars began to peel back the layers of

78

development of the Gospel and Epistle material. Burnett Hillman Streeter, New Testament scholar at Queen's College, Oxford, offered what he called a 'four-document hypothesis' for the Gospels: Matthew and Luke shared the two sources Mark and Q ('Quelle' for 'source', the hypothetical source of those passages where the two Gospels show a similarity to each other but not to Mark). Matthew and Luke also had, in addition, their own private sources: L (Lucan) and M (Matthew's). John was regarded as a special entity, apart from the 'Synoptic' gospels, and some observers saw it as being permeated with Hellenistic modes of thinking. There are many variations and elaborations of Streeter's basic analysis,[140] and this is of course but a curt introduction to a very complicated study. A 'quest for the historical Jesus' ensued in German theological scholarship which was later followed by the dramatic 'demythologizing' of Rudolf Bultmann.

To uncover the earliest stratum of Christian belief, Bultmann joined other German scholars in perfecting a method called 'form criticism' which examined the New Testament with the intention of discerning the various stylised forms of oral tradition behind it. Distinguishing among these traditions would help determine how faith built up the experiences of the early Christians into formulae which Bultmann, to the horror of fundamentalists, termed 'myths'. Demythologizing was Bultmann's process of getting beneath the myths to the believers' experiences. There are many critics, and not only those belonging to the fundamentalist camp, who today take issue with these methods, but the general approach of most Christians towards Holy Writ was radically changed. Roman Catholics still operated largely from the dictums of the sixteenth-century Council of Trent, which was fiercely dogmatic on the subject of biblical truth. Pius XII's 1943 encyclical, *Divino Afflante Spiritu*, with its encouragement of new biblical research and literary criticism changed that, and within a decade Rome had moved almost a quickly as had Protestants in a century.

The Protestant fundamentalists – especially in the United States – did not give up the struggle. Many broke away from the liberal-inclined denominations and felt vindicated by the successes their groups received with the evangelical and 'born-again' revivals of the 1960s and 70s. They were able to point out with glee that their memberships and contributions were up while the main-line denominations were experiencing a continued erosion of influence. Fundamentalists – with new names and organisations – were able to make their weight felt in the campaigns of Jimmy Carter and

Ronald Reagan, and through a hotchpotch of politico-religious pressure groups they began to legislate morality and attack the use of Darwin's evolutionary theories in public school classrooms.

For many American Christians, the Scopes trial of 1925 brought to a head the matter of literal interpretation of scripture. Intended as a test of civil liberties, the sensational nature of what transpired in Dayton, Tennessee, pitted the popular politician and darling of the fundamentalists, William Jennings Bryan, against the most famous criminal lawyer of his generation, Clarence Darrow, an agnostic. The charge was that John Thomas Scopes, a science teacher, had violated Tennessee law, which prohibited the teaching in public schools of any theories that denied the divine creation as taught in the Bible. The case might have been swiftly settled had not Bryan made the mistake of letting Darrow place him on the witness stand and cross-examine him on his beliefs regarding fundamentalist attitudes on biblical authority and science. A brilliant portrayal of that confrontation is presented in Lawrence and Lee's play *Inherit the Wind*, which provides a classic display of the Achilles' heel of any kind of fundamentalism.[141]

Drummond (Darrow) has shown Brady (Bryan) fossil remains of a prehistoric marine animal from Tennessee 'which lived here millions of years ago, when these mountain ranges were submerged in water'. Brady responds:

'I know. The Bible gives a fine account of the flood. But your professor is a little mixed up with his dates. That rock is no more than six thousand years old.' The play continues:

DRUMMOND: How do you know?

BRADY: A fine Biblical scholar, Bishop Ussher has determined for us the exact date and hour of the Creation. It occurred in the Year 4004 BC.

DRUMMOND: That's Bishop Ussher's opinion.

BRADY: It is not an opinion. It is literal fact, which the good Bishop arrived at through careful computation of the ages of the prophets as set down in the Old Testament. In fact, he determined that the Lord began the Creation on the 23rd of October in the Year 4004 BC at – uh, 9 a.m.!

DRUMMOND: That Eastern Standard Time? Or Rocky Mountain Time? It wasn't daylight-saving time, was it? Because the Lord didn't make the sun until the fourth day!

BRADY: That is correct.

80

DRUMMOND: That first day. Was it a twenty-four-hour day?
BRADY: The Bible says it was a day.
DRUMMOND: There wasn't any sun. How do you know how long it was?
BRADY: The Bible says it was a day.
DRUMMOND: A normal day, a literal day, a twenty-four-hour day?
BRADY: I do not know.
DRUMMOND: What do you think?
BRADY: I do not think about things that ... I do not think about!
DRUMMOND: Do you ever think about things that you *do* think about? Isn't it possible that first day was twenty-five hours long? There was no way to measure it, no way to tell! *Could* it have been twenty-five hours?
BRADY: It is ... *possible* ... (The production notes indicate that 'Drummond's got him. And he knows it! This is the turning point'.)
DRUMMOND: Oh. You interpret that the first day recorded in the Book of Genesis could be of indeterminate length.
BRADY: I mean to state that the day referred to is not necessarily a twenty-four-hour day.
DRUMMOND: It could have been thirty hours! Or a month! Or a year! Or a hundred years! (He brandishes the rock underneath Brady's nose) Or *ten million years*!

Many fundamentalists are conscious of this Achilles' heel: any admission that the biblical words might be interpreted in a 'larger' or figurative sense brings down the whole edifice. Some Christian fundamentalists today, however, do not accept Brady's type of literalism, and such matters as how old the earth is and how long the creating 'days' are are left open to question. Literal interpretation of the virgin birth and the miracles of Jesus is another matter: these are beyond questioning, and dissecting the Bible into various strata is also unacceptable.

Christians who have become accustomed to 'the quest for the historical Jesus', 'demythologizing', *The Passover Plot*, 'God is Dead' and *The Myth of God Incarnate*[142] are surprised that Muslims have not faced any similar onslaught. For Muslims, the Koran is the *ipsissima verba* of God himself, Allah's un-created speech: it is God speaking to man, not merely in the Arabia of the seventh century but from all eternity to every man throughout the world. The Koran, mediated to Muhammad

81

through the angel Gabriel as Allah's literal Word, is an article of faith; and in the words of Alfred Guillaume: 'The few who have questioned it have for the most part expressed their doubts in enigmatic language, so as to leave themselves a way of retreat from a dangerous position'.[143]

In the first and second Muslim centuries we hear of the Mu'tazilites, who were said to have attempted 'a justification of Islam in rational and philosophical terms. This led them to argue that reason was an equal source, with divine revelation, of moral truth'. Edward Mortimer goes on to describe their concept of God as 'a highly abstract one. They explained away all anthropomorphic descriptions of Him in the Koran ... as mere figures of speech. Rejecting the notion that the Koran was the eternal, "uncreated" Word of God, they insisted that He had created it in a specific time and place, for a specified purpose.'[144] Hamilton Gibb, however, warns against a description of the Mu'tazilites as rationalists and free-thinkers as our information about them was until recently from orthodox (therefore hostile) sources, and subsequent Mu'tazilite records modify the picture usually given of them in textbooks.[145]

In the past two centuries Muslim thinkers who have leaned toward a liberal interpretation of the Koran have been termed 'modernist', and one notable example in the nineteenth century was the pro-Western reformer of India, Sir Sayyid Ahmad Khan. He had reread the Koran in the light of the Western scientific thinking of his day and concluded, much like Western Christian writers earlier in the century, that there was no argument between divine revelation and natural law. Sayyid Ahmad Khan also challenged the orthodox view that the Koran was the 'eternal and uncreated Word of God'. His influence did much to remove British discrimination against Indian Muslims, but at the same time further isolated them from their Hindu compatriots. There were a number of Muslim writers earlier in this century – especially in Egypt– who were labelled 'modernist', but there has never been in Islam a movement or debate at all comparable to the Christian wrestling over biblical inerrancy and the literal interpretation of scripture.

There are a number of isolated Muslim scholars today who seem willing to enter the discussion of a literalist interpretation of the Koran: most notably, Muhammad Arkoun, an Algerian professor teaching in Paris, whose *Lectures du Coran* was published recently.[146] Arkoun deals with the problem of the divine authenticity of the Koran and the idea of the 'marvellous' in the holy book. He is not interested in what he calls an 'illusory reconciliation' between faith and reason and revelation and science, but rather in an exegesis which will explore 'the semiotic status of Koranic discourse' and 'the unveiling of the real stakes of historicity'. As Bernard Lewis said in his critique of the book: 'Arkoun is dissatisfied with the mere reiteration of the eternal verity of the Koran, but is not prepared to abandon it for a new secularism.'[147]

The Koran would never be treated in the same manner as was the Bible in the Scopes trial. 'Modernism', in the current climate of Islam, is a bad word. In a recently published booklet, *Muslims in Europe*, the imam of the London Central Mosque describes the modernist movement as that which 'came under the impact of European ideas and values', and he explains that this is what happened 'when students and trainees came into close contact with the Western way of life ... they came to associate everything wrong [in their lives] with Islamic society and the Islamic way of life'.[148]

Many Muslim writers feel that the work of 'higher criticism' has rendered the Christian scriptures unreliable. As Kenneth Cragg has written: 'Not understanding the demand for utter scientific liberty behind such studies, the average Muslim conversant with them assumes that quite evidently even Christians are at sea over their scriptures.'[149]

Attempts have been made to trace sources and the development of religious ideas in the Koran, but they have all come from Western writers. This pursuit in Muslim eyes is, as Hamilton Gibb puts it, 'not only meaningless but blasphemous;[150] yet it was probably inevitable: 'Disciples of the Higher Criticism, having watched with fascinated admiration how their masters played havoc with the traditional sacrosanctity of the Bible, threw themselves with brisk enthusiasm into the congenial task of demolishing the Koran.'[151] This is probably an unfair indictment of the motives of many of those involved in the attempt to discover sources in the Koran, but it is generally accepted today that there was a dismissal of koranic truth by some nineteenth-century European scholars on the basis of rather limited assessments.

The pursuit is usually seen as beginning in 1833 with the youthful work of Abraham Geiger, *Was hat Mohammed aus dem Judenthume aufgenommen?* ('What has Muhammad taken from Judaism?').[152] C. C. Torrey[153] returned to the argument of Jewish influences on the development of the Koran exactly a hundred years later. He tried to prove that Muhammad's knowledge of Christianity came from Jews rather than Christians, which explained why Muhammad has 'a Jewish attitude' towards Jesus. Tor Andrae[154] and K. Ahrens[155] indicated a strong Christian background. The possibilities seemed limitless as more writers started looking for sources. J. Finkel[156] found the missing link in non-rabbinic or pre-rabbinic Jewish sects; Gaster saw a Samaritan influence upon Muhammad;[157] and, most recently, Hebrew University professor Chaim Rabin has linked Islam with remnants of the Qumran sect.[158] There have been attempts to indicate the influence of Judaeo-Christian sects, like the Ebionites and Elkesaites, on Muhammad (see Chapter 1). The evidence of Gnostic traits in the Koran – the infancy stories and the denial of Jesus' Crucifixion – led C. Clemens in 1921 to see Manichaeism as having a decisive influence on Islam.[159]

Some attempts to unravel and explain Muhammad's religious background have been particularly offensive to Muslims. In *The Loom of History*, Herbert J. Muller presents a full gamut of this approach:

On his own heart had been inscribed more than Arab tradition. There were large numbers of Jews and Christians in Arabia, including many converted Arabs ... Mohammed had direct relations with colonies of Jews in and about Medina. In the Koran he displayed an acquaintance with their Scriptures, if an imperfect one (he declared that the Jews worshipped Ezra as the son of God) ... Of Christian Scriptures he had a more limited, garbled knowledge, or at least he felt freer to reinterpret them, in an original and somewhat incongruous fashion. Thus he denied the divinity of Christ and rejected the Crucifixion as a Jewish falsehood, while for some reason he accepted the miraculous birth ... he identified Allah with the God of Judaism and Christianity. He borrowed other ideas foreign to Arab tradition, notably the Last Judgment and the resurrection of the flesh, which the Arabs of Mecca thought ridiculous and revolting. We cannot know to what extent he consciously borrowed, and may assume that he was more deeply indebted than he realised.[160]

The idea of 'borrowing' and using 'multilated and confused versions' of biblical stories has been a popular one among Western writers. This pursuit has included speculation concerning certain clues the Koran seems to give. Sura 25 has 'the unbelievers' of Mecca asking, 'This [the Koran] is but a forgery of his own invention, in which others have helped him.' They also say, 'Fables of the ancients he has written: they are dictated to him morning and evening.' Sura 16.103 contains the words 'We know that they say: "A mortal taught him." But the man to whom they allude speaks a foreign tongue, while this [the Koran] is eloquent Arabic speech'.

Any number of candidates have been presented for the man who 'speaks a foreign tongue' from whom Muhammad possibly received his knowledge of Christian and Jewish tradition. The Meccans made a great objection to the authority of the revelation Muhammad presented to them: he was illiterate, and the local people felt he must have had one or more assistants in the 'forgery'. Jews and Christians of various persuasions could be found in the Arabia of Muhammad's day. In most cases they seemed to know little about their faith, for most of them were traders, butchers, smiths, pedlars, adventurers and slaves.

It is not known when the Gospels were first translated into Arabic; the oldest fragments date from the ninth century. Unless one accepts John Bowman's view that Muhammad was literate and influenced by the Syrian Diatessaron (see Chapter 3), one is left with exploring a number of possible individual and sectarian influences. The individual possibilities which have been presented include Waraqa, cousin of Khadija, Muhammad's wife; the slave Zaid, who belonged to a Christian tribe in southern Syria; a former Zoroastrian, Salman the Persian; and one of Muhammad's concubines, Mariyah, who was a Coptic Christian. There are accounts of the young Muhammad meeting Christian monks on his travels; and at the age of twelve, he once heard a sermon by the Bishop of Najran, Kos (also Qais). Most scholars would probably agree with Geoffrey Parrinder's assessment of these individual influences: 'all these are vague links and it is unlikely that there was much Christian teaching imparted through them'.[161]

We know that Muhammad visited Syria, first as a youth in the company of his uncle and later in the service of his future wife. The link with that country is seen as an important one by a number of scholars. There were Jews and Christians organised into communities in the north, south and east of Arabia, and the Christian groups were principally Monophysite or Nestorian. The latter faith with its well-known missionary zeal, was especially active, and the town of Hira on the Euphrates was the see of a Nestorian bishop. Muhammad's debates with southern Arabian Christians are well documented, but many scholars place more emphasis on the influence of Syrian Christians – mainly because of the heavy Syriac influence in the Koran.

85

It is estimated that of the 'foreign language' influences in the Koran, Syriac accounts for 70%. This compares to the Hebrew and Greek/Latin influences, which amount to 10% each. As noted earlier, John Bowman sees a striking similarity between the koranic listing of Old Testament personages and that of the Syrian Diatessaron, and there is not a single biblical name with an exclusively Hebrew pronunciation in the Koran.[162] Such words as 'glorify', 'fast', 'sacrifice', 'Christ', 'Kingdom of God' are all presented in their Syriac form.

W. Montgomery Watt has commented that 'When one turns to questions of detail, one finds that the particular Jewish and Christian groups which influenced the Arabs must have had many strange ideas.' He is not referring to the heterodoxy of the Nestorians or the Monophysites; he is thinking of the 'extraordinary ideas derived from apocryphal gospels ... that seem to have been floating about Arabia'. There is an ancient saying, *Arabia haeresium ferax* ('Arabia fertile in heresies'), and Watt gives the example of the koranic passage (Sura 5.116) which suggests that the Trinity consists of the Father, the Son and the Virgin Mary. This is 'doubtless a criticism of some nominally Christian Arabs who held this view'.[163] The Arabian Christian sects, the Mariamites and Collyridians whose cult was said to 'verge on idolatry', are a possible source for this.

Examples of parallels of the Koran to clearly Gnostic-style stories were given earlier (see page 35), and the possibility of influences from Gnostic groups and other religious bodies on the periphery of Judaism and Christianity cannot be excluded if one undertakes the search for 'sources'. One of the most thorough, yet restrained, analyses along this line was made by the Swedish scholar Tor Andrae in 1936. Andrae, like other observers, begins his study by indicating similarities between Syrian Christianity and certain aspects of koranic thought. The form and style of Muhammad's preaching as well as his devotional exercises seem to echo those of Syrian monks and hermits:

'The deep earnestness, the keen expectation of future life, the contrition and trembling before the day of judgement, fear as an actual proof of piety, the warning against carelessness which forgets responsibility and retribution: these things form also the basic mood of *Christian ascetic* piety as it survived in the Oriental churches.'[164]

The similarities between the Koran's description of judgement and sermons preached by the celebrated father of the Syrian Church, St. Ephraim, were noted by Andrae. One point in particular he assigns to a Nestorian background: Muhammad's idea that the soul sinks into complete unconsciousness after death so that the day of judgement seems to follow immediately after death (see the Koran 6.93f; 56.82f; 75.26f). He says, 'At that time such an idea existed only in the Nestorian church.'[165]

Andrae is careful to stress that such ideas entered Muhammad's thinking as impressions: 'He was conscious of no premeditation. Does this mean that none such was present? Assuredly not. The spirit of inspiration does not function in a vacuum. It employs the assembled material that the soul already possesses, whether actually in the consciousness or hidden and concealed in the dark subconscious.'[166] It is certain that Muhammad received no full appreciation of the Christian faith: there is in the Koran no understanding at all of the sacraments, the Christian cult with all its festivals or the priesthood. Kenneth Cragg has wisely reminded us concerning this point: 'The Qur'an took up and laid the sanction – and sanctity – of Divine revelation upon misunderstandings for which the Church must bear its measure of responsibility. Misconceptions as to the Trinity and Jesus make clear that Muhammad was never in a position to know at first hand the authentic Christianity of the New Testament.'[167]

Andrae sees other influences, stressing the point that Muhammad's conception of revelation – 'living and actual' rather than the 'eternal and unchangeable' tradition of orthodox Judaism and Christianity – 'betrays a relationship' to what he terms 'Ebionite-Manichaean doctrine'. Muhammad 'was influenced, even if he was not actually awakened, by the struggle for religious independence which had given Mani and the Gnostics such a strong position among the people of the Orient ... We understand why he ... never gave a thought to the possibility of becoming a Christian. He already knew, from the echo of the Gnostic-Manichaean theory of revelation which had reached his ears, that Christendom was only one among other similarly privileged communities which had experienced Divine guidance and revelation.'[168]

The possibility of a direct or indirect influence stemming from Gnostic sources has usually been played down on the grounds that 'Gnostic sects had completely died out by the end of the fifth century.'[169] Nazir Ahmad's 'completely died out' is not quite accurate: the heyday of most Gnostic groups had been the second and third centuries, and the main thrust had dissipated by the time Muhammad began to preach, but the influence had been channelled into different directions by the sixth and seventh centuries. Manichaeism, the last great Gnostic sect, continued to exert a limited influence in the Near East after the fourth and fifth centuries, and the geographer Rustah reports the arrival of Manichaean missionaries at Mecca from Hira.

Mani's religion is an extremely complicated matter, but briefly it is known he was born at Seleucia-Ctesiphon, capital of the Persian empire, in the third century, and it is likely his father was a member of the Mandaean or Elkesaite sect. His system was a hotchpotch of long-dead heresies, but, like Muhammad, he saw himself as a new and final prophet in the line of many before him: both stressed the doctrines of judgement and 'last things' and lacked a detailed knowledge of orthodox Christianity; both were highly critical of Judaism; both were strongly missionary and universalist in approach; and both denied the Incarnation and Crucifixion of Jesus. A. A. Bevan noted many years ago that the koranic denial of the Crucifixion was a 'striking analogy' to the Manichaean view.[170]

I have always been fascinated by the mention in the Koran of a third 'people of the book' (with Christians and Jews), the Sabians. The Mandaeans of Iraq and Iran, the only Gnostic sect to survive into modern times, are still called the *Subba* by Arabic-speaking peoples. Their name means something like 'dippers', referring to their practice of oft-repeated immersions. The Mandaeans are usually identified in koranic commentaries as the Sabians of the Koran, but their origin is highly disputed and complicated. They believe their religion is primordial and founded in 'the world of light', and are totally unconcerned with the history of this world. The publication in 1953 by Lady Drower of the Mandaean *Haran Gawaita* scroll gave the interesting narration of a first-century exodus of Mandaeans from Palestine to Mesopotamia via Abraham's town of Harran. Scholars who argue for a Syro-Palestinian origin for the Mandaeans point to Mandaean affinities with Judaism. Yet the familiar antagonism towards Judaism that is found among the Ebionites and Elkesaites is also present in Mandaism; that odd collection of Judaeo-Christian sects across the River Jordan seems to have much in common with the Mandaeans. There are also Babylonian and Persian elements to the religion, making their tradition a difficult one to unravel[171].

The appellation 'Sabian', however, has not been exclusively identified with the Mandaean sect; there are also the famous

Harranian 'pseudo-Sabians' who translated so many classics into Arabic. The latter group, according to Lady Drower, are probably related to their simpler and more primitive brethren of the Tigris-Euphrates marshes, and this relationship is possibly indicated in the *Haran Gawaita* 'exodus' (via Harran).[172]

Richard Bell suggests that the koranic Sabians might be the Elkesaites who maintained themselves in the north-west of Arabia, where they would be known to the Meccans and may have even have exercised some influence upon Muhammad.[173] We noted in Chapter 1 A. W. F. Blunt's suggestion that Muhammad 'lived for some time in an Elkesaite community'.[174] At the 1973 International Colloquium on Gnosticism in Stockholm, Eric Segelberg asked if both Manichaeism and Mandaism were influenced by the Elkesaites.[175]

Even more intriguing than 'Sabian' is the earliest name the Mandaeans have for themselves, 'Nasoraeans'. It means 'observants' and has come to designate those 'adept in the mysteries of the religion' while 'Mandaean' ('Gnostic' in derivation) now signifies 'laymen' in the faith. The relationship of 'Nasoraean' to the koranic term for all Christians, *Nasara*, is an interesting possibility, especially since there seems no answer as to what that word originally meant or why it was chosen. It is Syriac in origin, and a great deal of scholarly ink has been spent indicating that the Syriac root has no affinity, as might be supposed, with 'Nazarene' (Nazareth). It remains a mystery, unless it has a meaning similar to the idea of the Mandaic 'Nasoraean'.[176]

The fourth-century heresiologist Epiphanius of Salamis precluded an identification of two Jewish groups he described with seemingly similar names, the *Nazoraioi* and the *Nasaraioi* (*Panarion*, 1.18). The former were Jewish Christians; the latter pre-Christian Jews dwelling along the Jordan, rejecting sacrifices but observing much of the Jewish law and possessing a concept of revelation which seems similar to Muhammad's. The *Nasaraioi*, like the Elkesaites who were in the same area, entertained an idea of revelation and prophecy as being living and actual, ongoing. As Andrae noted, Muhammad's doctrine of revelation could not have come from orthodox Judaism or Christianity. His concept of the scriptures was like that of the Nasaraioi and Elkesaites: dynamic, not static. Like Mani, he excluded the writing prophets from consideration in his list of previous prophets of Allah. We also know that the Elkesaite Book of Elxai alludes to a concept of Christ as being often born on earth, at different times and in different

89

forms.[177] Muhammad's idea of a particular revelation for each people seems related to this current of thought. Orthodox Jews and Christians were only groups among many experiencing divine guidance and revelation. Muhammad realised that every people had its prophet – where was the one for the Arabs? Islam would become a religion going back to the pure monotheism of Abraham, which was neither Christian nor Jewish.

The Mandaeans were careful in their history to distinguish themselves from the Byzantine Christians, the *Kristiyane*, whom they despised for practising baptism with non-flowing water. An ancient inscription at Naqsh-i-Rustam enumerating the non-Zoroastrian sects persecuted by the Zoroastrian authorities shows the same distinction between *Kristiyane* and *Nasoraye*. One is tempted to speculate that Muhammad may have been perpetuating an important distinction by his choice of *Nasara* for Christians in the Koran.

The Mandaeans, with their combination of Babylonian and Persian cultic practices, bizarre Gnostic mythology and Christian and Jewish affinities, possess a truly unique culture. They are a remarkable link to the genesic days of both Christianity and Islam, but as the East German Mandaean scholar Kurt Rudolph has said: 'It is tragic that (our understanding of the Mandaeans) is happening at a time when this exceptional religion is moving toward its end, a movement which, according to the Mandaean religion itself, is towards the Kingdom of Life and Light, for which Mandaeans have always longed.'[178]

I have sensed for some time that there is much worth exploring in the 'Mandaean connection', and would like to see the possible ramifications of their remarkable culture investigated more openly than has thus far been the case. The Mandaean tradition has been the preserve of obscure and rarefied academic journals where the discussion of their value frequently sinks into a sea of impossible semantics. Unfortunately, the Mandaean tradition has become a theological football for some scholars in the discussion of whether there was a well-developed Gnostic tradition before the Christian era.[179]

John Wansbrough, Reader in Arabic at the University of London, has indicated the pitfalls of the search for 'sources' and links between Muhammad and various religious systems: 'the simple collation of phenomena common to two or more confessions in the monotheist tradition is seldom adequate to more than demonstration of the equally simple assertion that a confessional community belonging to the Judaeo-Christian tradition must exhibit some, and probably will exhibit other traditional features.' The example he criticised was that of Chaim Rabin that some late remnants of the Qumran sect survived until the time of Muhammad. It is beyond the scope of this volume to enter into this particular debate, but Wansbrough's point is important for any of the 'searches' given by scholars: 'the method of selected parallels is of virtually unlimited application but also likely to be productive of little more than tautologies.'[180]

A critic even more sweeping in his analysis is A. L. Tibawi, who has written two *Critiques of English-speaking Orientalists and Their Approach to Islam and the Arabs*. For any observer of the difficulties which exist between those who yearn for a more open dialogue between the Judaeo-Christian and Islamic traditions, these volumes should be required reading. Tibawi is scathing in his attack on those who have asserted that 'Islam is an imperfect or distorted form of Christianity' or that 'the Qur'an shows dependence on Biblical tradition'. He assails a number of very influential British orientalists and asks some pointed questions: Why there is no reciprocal Christian recognition of Muhammad as a prophet? Is it any business of Western observers to suggest a change in the spirit of Islam? Why is it that works like the *Encyclopaedia of Islam* carry almost no articles from Arab contributors?[181] There is much more, but one is left with no doubt that Western attempts to approach the Koran with the same tools of criticism which have been applied to the Jewish and Christian scriptures will receive a very negative response: the nature of the overture itself is wrong.

Alfred Guillaume, who is of the school of Western orientalists that Tibawi takes to task, addressed himself to the question of the effect of modern historical criticism on Muslims in his comprehensive volume *Islam*. He concluded there was a 'small but by no means negligible, minority' of those who have been 'students at universities with a Western tradition who have an understanding of these things'. Many such students in conversation with the author took 'an unorthodox view of the Quran and a highly critical view of tradition ... But to treat the Quran as the writing of a man, even of an inspired man, is more than they dare attempt: the power of the *'ulama* (mullah) is too much for them, and no position in the public service would be open, or would remain open, to them if they expressed doubt about the Quran being literally the Word of God.'[182] He proceeds to give a number of excruciating examples where this has occurred.

Western observers find this difficult to comprehend, but we are daily confronted with even more hair-raising examples coming from the Iran of the Ayatollah Khomeini. Most Christians have been able to withstand suggestions that the Dead Sea Scrolls discovery indicated that the Essene Teacher of Righteousness was a prototype for Christ, or that John's Gospel was filled with the alien intrusion of Hellenistic philosophy. The Mandaean scholar Rudolf Macuch asserted, 'The Gospel of John is so saturated with Mandaean elements that these can be unperceived only by one who is blind.'[183] This is to say nothing of the popular influence of such books as *The Nazarene Gospel Restored, The Sacred Mushroom* or *The Holy Blood and the Holy Grail*[184] presented to the public by reputable publishers as serious historical contributions. One wonders what reaction there would be in Islam if an archaeological discovery were made proving that Muhammad had spent his formative years in a Gnostic community – would it be destroyed if it were uncovered in a Muslim land?

Christian and Jewish biblical scholars insist that a better understanding of how the scriptures were written is a boon rather than an obstacle to faith. To most biblical scholars, demands by fundamentalists for inerrancy are beside the point. The differences, even the contradictions, between the Gospel accounts do not detract from the spiritual truths that they contain; if anything, they give us a better understanding of the world in which they were written. 'God can reveal himself through inspired fiction, like the story of Jonah, just as well as through inspired history,'[185] said Father Raymond Brown while professor of New Testament studies at my seminary, Union in New York.

R. C. Zaehner, one-time professor of eastern religions at Oxford, felt in 1958 that the same process would eventually be extended by Muslims to the Koran:

> No doubt sooner or later this operation will have to be faced; and when it happens it may well have a more shattering effect on Islam than ever it had on Christianity: but so long as Muslims continue to believe that the Qur'an is what tradition claims it to be, no argument from the Christian side is likely to have the slightest effect.[186]

There seems little likelihood in the present mood of Islam that Muslims will move in this direction; a question which will be discussed in Chapter 8 is whether indeed they should. Should

Christians and Jews try to impose their own understanding of scriptures upon Muslims? Orthodox opinion has rigidly maintained that the Koran, apart from questions of literary criticism, is 'untranslatable, a miracle of speech which it would be blasphemous to imitate'.

This attitude toward the Koran is hard to reconcile with the continued use of *The Gospel of Barnabas*, which so blatantly contradicts Muhammad's revelation on several points. It is this inconsistency which makes fundamentalism so exasperating. Orthodox Muslims, on the one hand, bitterly denounce the claims of Mirza Ghulam Ahmad, the founder of the Ahmadi Muslims, and yet gladly accept a blatant forgery his sect has made so readily available to the Muslim world. They decry critical methods of interpretation being applied to the Koran, yet make polemical use of the results of those methods when applied to the Judaeo-Christian scriptures. It is a strange historical twist that Fra Marino's odd exercise in revenge should be issued today from Lahore and other Muslim centres as 'the most authentic Gospel'.

CHAPTER SIX

'Nor Did They Crucify Him': the Koranic Denial of Jesus' Crucifixion

'Judas answered [the high priest]: "I have told you that I am Judas Iscariot, who promised to give into your hands Jesus the Nazarene; and ye, by what art I know not, are beside yourselves, for ye will have it by every means that I am Jesus."' (*The Gospel of Barnabas*, Chapter 217). The portrait of Judas in *Barnabas* magically transformed into his Master's likeness so 'that his disciples and believers entirely believed that he was Jesus' is an odd one, but not one of the twelve has attracted as many accretions and interpretations over the centuries. Christians have always had a rather caricature view of the betrayer: a 'Judas' has become a feature of our popular vocabulary as one who deceives under the guise of friendship. In Dante's *Inferno*, he is placed in the deepest chasm of hell.

There is surprisingly little about Judas in the gospel material. In the Synoptic Gospels he does not appear until the Passion narrative, and John has only two brief mentionings earlier. In the lists of apostles Judas comes last, with the qualifying epithets: 'who betrayed him' and 'who became a traitor'. *The Gospel of Barnabas* carries John's judgement that Judas was possessed by a devil. In the apocryphal Gospel of the Infancy, the child Jesus drives out of the child Judas a devil in the form of a dog.

Judas' name 'Iscariot' implies that, unlike the other twelve, he was from Judaea and comes from the Hebrew, meaning 'man of Kerioth', a village in the Judaean hills. Ronald Brownrigg has suggested that 'As a Judaean he might well have been a more sophisticated, more shrewd and more dispassionate character among a bunch of rustic, emotional and impassioned Galileans'.[187] Judas has been viewed as the odd man out: jealous of Galilean rivals, especially the inner circle of Peter, James and John. A great deal has been written as to Judas' motive in the betrayal. John gives a hint (12.6) which is not supported by the Synoptics. Judas criticises Mary of Bethany for wasting 300 denarii of perfume with which she anointed Jesus' feet. Judas asks, 'Why was this perfume not sold for thirty pounds and given to the poor?' John adds that 'He said this, not out of care for the poor, but because he was a thief; he used to pilfer the money put into the common purse, which was in his charge'. Another view was advanced by Thomas de Quincey early in the nineteenth century that Judas was a high-minded individual who wished to compel Jesus to declare his messiahship and thus hasten the inauguration of the Kingdom of God.

As we have seen, sympathy for Judas was given by that bizarre Gnostic sect the Cainites, who were said to have used a Gospel of Judas fragments of which indicate a favourable evaluation of the betrayer. The canonical Gospels almost give the feeling that Judas has been assigned the role of villain to play in the drama of the Passion. *The Gospel of Barnabas* carries this to the extreme where he is the willing and plotting betrayer: 'When the lamb was eaten (Passover), the devil came upon the back of Judas, and he went forth from the house, Jesus saying to him again: "Do quickly that which thou must do."' Later, Judas 'impetuously' enters the room from which Jesus had been taken up by the angels and is transformed into Jesus' appearance. After his arrest, he protests his innocence and 'speaks many words of madness', telling Pilate 'if thou put me to death, thou shalt do a great wrong'.

There are a number of accounts the author of *Barnabas* could have used in creating his substitution story. It is, of course, not known from what exact source Muhammad derived the idea that Jesus did not die on the cross, and it is uncertain in what sense this denial (in Sura 4.156f) should be taken. Muslim commentators on the Koran have offered a variety of possibilities, and the prevalent, but by no means exclusive, opinion has been that someone or other was substituted for Jesus.

The fourteenth-century cosmographer Mba (al-Dimaski) maintains that Judas assumed the likeness of Jesus and was crucified in his place. Baidawi, the learned thirteenth-century jurist and exegete whose commentary has been regarded by Sunni Muslims almost as a holy book, gives one interpretation which is similar at several points to the scenario in *Barnabas*:

> 'It is related that a group of Jews reviled Isa and his mother, who in turn cursed them. Allah turned the Jews into monkeys and swine. Then the Jews gathered to kill him. Whereupon Allah informed him that he would take him up to heaven. Then Isa said to his disciples, "Which one of you is willing to have my likeness cast upon him, and be killed and crucified and enter Paradise?" One of them accepted, and Allah cast the likeness of Isa upon him, and he was killed and crucified. It is said also that he was one who acted the hypocrite toward Isa, and went out to lead the Jews to him. But Allah cast the likeness of Isa upon him, and he was taken and crucified and killed.[188]

Judas is not named as the victim, but there seems little doubt that he is the one implied.

The equally influential ninth-century commentator, Tabari, gives several possible interpretations, including 'a Jewish chief called Joshua' who was given the form and appearance of Jesus and crucified in his place despite his protests. As previously noted, Tabari also has a point repeated in *Barnabas* of Jesus descending from heaven to his mother and disciples to explain what has really happened. Tabari quotes accounts given earlier by the Arab story-teller of Persian descent, Wahb ibn Munabbih. This seventh-century writer apparently had a number of contacts with learned Jews and Christians in his native district, and sometimes his comments were in complete agreement with theirs.

One account, attributed to Wahb and given by an author of the tenth-century, Tha'labi, is similar to Baidawi's and Dimaski's[189] commentaries in naming Judas as Jesus' substitute:

> Then they put up a tree in order to crucify him. When they brought him to the tree to crucify, *darkness covered the earth, and God sent angels who stood between them and Jesus. The shape of Jesus was cast upon Judas who had pointed him out, and they crucified him instead, thinking he was Jesus.* After three hours God took Jesus to Himself and lifted him up to heaven ... *When he who was similar to Jesus was crucified,* Mary, the mother of Jesus and a woman ... came to weep. But Jesus came and said ... God has lifted me up ... and this is merely *a person who* was made to appear similar to them.[190]

According to Samuel Stern, the portions in italics were those added by Tha'labi to an original text of Wahb which is given by Tabari. This text speaks of 'something which was made to appear similar to them', and Stern thinks it was interpolated by Tha'labi by exchanging the phantom 'something' for a substitute, Judas, to bring it into line with 'the common version' of the time: 'the idea of this miraculous substitute for Jesus was the most common interpretation of the koranic verse, whereas the idea of a "phantom" is unusual.'[191]

With Tha'labi's version we may be near, if not at the very beginning, of the Muslim tradition of Judas as Jesus' substitute – perhaps it was the account employed by the author of *Barnabas*. Wahb's stories were very popular among Muslims and greatly utilised in polemical writings. Other early Muslim exegetes merely stated, without giving details, that 'someone' was substituted for Jesus. There are a number of traditions with the notion that one of the apostles was turned into the shape of Jesus and volunteered to give himself up in place of the Master. Another version attributed to Wahb has seventeen apostles who all miraculously assumed the shape of Jesus and of which one sacrificed himself. Ibn Ishaq, whose biography became the standard work on the subject, names a thirteenth apostle, Sergius, as being the one crucified in Jesus' place.

Jabbar's tenth-century book the *Signs of Muhammad's Prophecy*, which Shlomo Pines suggested contained lost records of Judaeo-Christian material, is an extremely useful document in a different direction: it illustrates some of the earliest Muslim polemical views, and their likely sources. Jabbar contends that, just as the Koran says, the Christian religion is different from that taught by Jesus: Christians themselves differed from the official line developed by the credal Church. Given his polemical stance, it was natural that Jabbar should utilise an apocryphal Passion account which seems to him to have Judas kissing the wrong man and another taking Jesus' place on the cross (see page 20). Stern thinks it likely that rather than being an early Christian variant of the Passion as maintained by Jabbar, it is 'an account made by a Muslim author out of vague reminiscences of the gospel story, just as Wahb and Ibn Ishaq had made up such accounts'.[192]

Jabbar uses the same method elsewhere in his writing, and the style of *Barnabas* is frequently similar to this. Jabbar chooses a number of passages from the New Testament which he says show Jesus did not claim divinity (John 7.38; 8.40; 14.24; 17.3; Matthew

97

10.28; 19.16–17; Luke 12.13–14; among others). Passages in which Jesus is said to have claimed divinity for himself are either forgeries or can be satisfactorily explained: 'Son of God' is not to be taken literally but metaphorically. Jabbar says of the latter category: 'There were Christians who saw the light and became Muslims; when they examined the passages and expressions which the Christians pretend the Messiah used.' Stern thinks this passage gives us the clue that 'Abd al-Jabbar was indebted for the information ... to Christian converts to Islam'. The same method was used by the ninth-century Ali ibn Rabban al-Tabari, a Christian physician converted late in his life to Islam. Two of his books became 'arsenals to provide Muslim apologists with passages from the Old and New Testaments allegedly containing prophecies about the future coming of Muhammad'.[193]

The author of *Barnabas* knew this 'pick and choose' procedure well, as we have seen. Jabbar does not say where he finds another polemical piece he employs, information about Christians decrying the virgin birth of Jesus: 'His aim in quoting it is to show Christians in as bad a light as possible: the Muslims believe in the virgin birth – whereas there are some Christians who deny it.'[194] This was the same argument he used with the Crucifixion account. Stern shows, convincingly, how most of this material is from ex-Christian Muslims. Tabari also describes the Judas' substitution story as being the opinion of certain Christians who were also possibly converts to Islam. The polemic we see in the Gospel of Barnabas and continued into our day in various Muslim centres is rooted in these early discussions, and we are taken further back to the formative days of koranic interpretation than many observers have previously supposed. Many modern Muslim polemical tracts repeat almost word for word the same line of argument we find in Jabbar's tenth-century work.

In his 1968 analysis of Jabbar, Stern gives the opinion that 'the conclusion that another person was crucified instead of Jesus fits very well the main trend of Islamic tradition. The exact meaning of the koranic passage is by no means certain; what is clear is that Muhammad has adopted a docetic doctrine.' An interesting argument is used by Jabbar that 'were the Prophet an impostor, he would have thought twice before denying the crucifixion in the teeth of the assertions of both Jews and Christians, especially since he aimed at gaining their adherence [to his revelation]'. But, as Stern adds, 'This is all well and good but Christians do not feel the crucifixion is based on a matter of opinion'.[195]

Like that of other Gnostics, the Docetist Christians' (see page 17) attitude towards matter as 'alien to the supreme God' required the rejection of any genuine Incarnation. It was inconceivable that the divine Christ could have come 'in the flesh': the humanity and sufferings of the earthly Christ were apparent rather than real. The Islamic philosophy is matter-affirming, and theological opposition to Isa's crucifixion is that Allah would not allow one of his prophets to suffer the accursed death of the cross. The Gnostic reason for the rejection is quite different from the Muslim. This did not, however, stop Muslim commentators from finding support for the idea of a substitution in Gnostic teaching; in these accounts was ample proof of the variance Christians had regarding the issue. This approach is still found in polemical tracts today.

Polemical ammunition could be found in the teachings of Basilides, the famous Egyptian Gnostic Christian who lived in the second century. Like those of most Gnostics, his writings are known largely through the comments of his opponents, and these differ greatly. Irenaeus, the Church father quoted by 'Fra Marino' in the Spanish preface of *The Gospel of Barnabas*, says that Basilides taught that the divine Nous (Intelligence) appeared in human form in Christ but at the Crucifixion changed forms with Simon of Cyrene who had been pressed into service to carry Jesus' cross (Mark 15.21). It has been suggested that Basilides possibly took advantage of the stylistic ambiguity of this passage to develop his notion that Simon not only carried but suffered on Christ's cross. Basilides' account ends with a bizarre touch: 'Jesus, however, took on the form of Simon, and stood by laughing at them.' Christ's enemies are thus derided for their ignorance. A strikingly similar account is to be found in the Nag Hammadi text *The Second Treatise of the Great Seth*, unearthed in Upper Egypt in 1945. Jesus is recorded as saying: 'It was not I whom they struck with the reed. It was another who lifted up the cross onto his shoulders – Simon. It was another on whose head they placed the thorny crown. But I was up above, rejoicing over all ... And I was laughing at their ignorance.'[196] Mani called Jesus 'son of the widow', and seems to have thought that the son of the widow of Nain, whom Jesus had raised, was finally put to death in his place. Suggestions for substitutes in Muslim commentaries have included Simon of Cyrene and Pilate(!); and a Manichaean document taught that the devil, who was hoping to have Jesus crucified, himself fell a victim to the Crucifixion.

Modernist Muslim interpretations have not accepted the idea of substitution. A book by a well-known Egyptian doctor and writer, Muhammad Kamel Hussein[197] published in English as *City of Wrong* created a great deal of discussion because it purported to be 'the first ever written in the world of Islam, which makes a thorough study of the central theme of the Christian faith [the crucifixion]'. As Albert Hourani has said, 'the book itself is not about the crucifixion at all.'[198] Jesus does not die on the cross; and to Hussein it does not really matter whether Jesus was killed or not because his book is really an exploration of the motives of those who condemned Jesus and 'the endless struggle between the individual conscience and the immoral collective will'.[199] *City of Wrong* (the name refers to Jerusalem) reminds one of Good Friday three-hour homilies which look into the drama of the individuals and groups surrounding Christ's passion, having first removed what is the heart of the matter: his death on Calvary.

Hussein gives an interpretation of the koranic denial of Jesus' Crucifixion which is rarely seen in the new fundamentalist climate:

the idea of a substitute for Christ is a very crude way of explaining the Quranic text. They had to explain a lot to the masses. No cultured Muslim believes in this nowadays. The text is taken to mean that the Jews thought they killed Christ but God raised him unto Him in a way we can leave unexplained among the several mysteries we have taken for granted on faith alone.[200]

As Hussein suggests, it is important to note the context in which the denial is given in the Koran. The Dawood translation gives it as:

They (the Jews) denied the truth and uttered a monstrous falsehood against Mary. They declared: 'We have put to death the Messiah Jesus the son of Mary, the apostle of Allah.' They did not kill him, nor did they crucify him, but thought they did. Those who disagreed about him were in doubt concerning his death, for what they knew about it was sheer conjecture; they were not sure that they had slain him. Allah lifted him up to His presence; He is mighty and wise. There is none among the People of the Book but will believe in him before his death; and on the Day of Resurrection he will be a witness against them.[201]

A number of scholars have said the denial must be interpreted more as a defence against the Jews who maintained that they alone had killed and crucified Jesus. Ubayy ibn Ka'b, one of

Muhammad's secretaries, is said to have read into the passage: 'and they who entertained wrong opinions about him, did not crucify him'. 'They' are, of course, the Jews, and their assertion is an insult to Mary. Allah confounded them by lifting Jesus to his presence. The end of the passage seems to indicate that all must be brought to belief in Jesus and that he will witness concerning them at the resurrection. This has given rise to an extraordinary tradition, as we shall see in the next chapter.

A number of Christian writers have attempted interpretations of the text in the vein presented by Hussein. Zaehner says that *shubbiha* means, first, 'to cause to resemble' and, second, 'to cause doubt'. He feels that

> in the context it is more natural to take *shubbiha* in the sense of 'doubt was caused for them', for the following sentence ('And those who differ therein are in doubt because of him') seems to be a gloss on the unusual phrase. If, however, we take Jesus as the subject, we must translate, 'he was made a likeness to them', which seems meaningless unless it is a reference to some other text.[202]

Writing in 1923, E. E. Elder says that a free translation of *shubbiha lahum* ('he was made to resemble another for them') could be 'it was made a misunderstanding – a perplexity to them'. In that case, the verse could then be properly translated as: 'Yet they slew him not, and they crucified him not – but it (His Crucifixion) was made a misunderstanding to them.' Jesus' Crucifixion 'perplexed them'; they saw the event, but failed to appreciate its inner meaning.[203] A number of readings like those of Zaehner and Elder have been presented in order to bring the text more into line with the Christian Gospel, but these have not been accepted by Muslim writers.

A recent and extensive interpretation in this vein comes from the Italian Franciscan Giulio Basetti-Sani.[204] Basetti-Sani is a talented scholar, and has been associated with the noteworthy tradition of the Dominican Institute of Oriental Studies in Cairo which has produced such competent observers of Islam as Jacques Jomier and G. C. Anawati. At one time he was a member of a group in Cairo called *Badaliva*, a movement whose purpose was to manifest Jesus Christ in Islamic lands. On the surface, Basetti-Sani's book appears to be a great stride forward in bettering relations between Muslims and Christians. It gives a comprehensive survey of koranic theology and literary form, but the eventual intent is clear: a reading of the Koran 'in the light of Christ', that is the orthodox Christian Christ. We shall return to Basetti-Sani's approach in Chapter 8 because it has much to say about the future of dialogue between Christians and Muslims.

Basetti-Sani feels that 'before we reject the Koran entirely, because the ordinary interpretation by Muslims does not permit Catholics to see any authenticity in it, why should we not see whether another interpretation, made "with the light of Christ", might let us find what the Muslims have not succeeded in finding?' His reading of the koranic text on Jesus' death does just that, and his interpretation goes further than any Christian observer thus far: 'The statements of the Koran ... do not refer to the *fact of the crucifixion and death* of Jesus.' These statements deny that the *true perpetrators* of the deed were *Jews*! The koranic statement must be read and understood in the light of Christian dogma on the meaning and worth of the death of Christ. The death and Resurrection of Christ are proof of his divine mission, but they are even more the great mystery of God's mercy, which has a cosmic meaning and cannot be produced by men. Therefore the death of Jesus was not the result of the trial and condemnation of a supposed criminal, brought about by the religious authorities of Israel ('We killed the Messiah') and by the Roman authorities; it was an event preordained by God and executed by 'diabolical powers' which used men as mere tools to carry out the affair. The text must be interpreted against the background of Pauline thought: if the Jews are 'the enemies of the cross of Christ' (Galatians 6.12–14; Philippians 3.18), then the Crucifixion of Jesus is the effect of the machinations of the powers and the 'princes of this world'. Christ's death is part of the divine plan of Incarnation and redemption: the glorification of the Son of God. It is 'the wisdom of God, mysterious, hidden, which God foreordained before the world ... which none of the rulers of this world has known; for had they known it, they would never have crucified the Lord of glory' (I. Corinthians 2.7–8).

Basetti-Sani does not stop there:

Furthermore, the death of Christ was not caused by the condemnation of Jews and Romans. It was Jesus' free and spontaneous self-immolation. No one, except the Father and Jesus himself, could have disposed of his life ... Hence, in light of [the] gospel text and the Christian dogma on the free and

102

spontaneous self-immolation of Jesus, we must read and interpret the koranic text thus: No! It was not the Jews who killed and crucified Christ; he gave himself freely. Even after his death, during the hours that preceded his rising, Christ remained alive in some manner, in the sense expressed by the Roman [Catholic] liturgy for Holy Saturday: 'I have become like a man who needs no help, free among the dead.'[205]

Most koranic scholars would find Basetti-Sani's approach hard to swallow; Muslim fundamentalists would find it offensive. As we shall suggest in Chapter 8, despite the priest's obviously noble intentions this reading of the Koran is more of an insult to Muslims than is the old-fashioned polemical interpretation. Basetti-Sani is saying that only Christians – orthodox Catholic ones at that – can correctly interpret the Koran. Despite the ecumenical guise, his approach comes across, in the final analysis, in the same manner as Muslim polemicist suggestions that the Christian scriptures are corrupt and can only be read in the light of Muhammad.

The handsome new translation made of the Koran by Muhammad Asad to mark Islam's 1400th year (1979) commented on Sura 4.156f. as follows: 'Thus the Qur'an categorically denies the story of the crucifixion of Jesus.' The author does not proceed in his commentary to offer any theories, but the point here and elsewhere is that Muslims are not ready to see the kind of rereading of their sacred book being offered from Christian writers – and why should they?

The imam of the London Central Mosque, S. M. Darsh, writes for Muslims in Europe saying:

In the sphere of theology there is no giving up the battle ... Christians are accused of misunderstanding the true nature of Jesus as a human being, accepting the pagan conception of a human god, defamation of the Supreme Being in ascribing incarnation to Him, accepting unfounded myths about the crucifixion and seeking to justify it in a way which denigrates human nature.[206]

Ahmadi Muslim polemicists are even blunter:

[Christians] believe that Jesus actually died on the Cross but on the third day he rose up to the heavens. What a paradox! What a myth! Modern Christianity rests on the belief that Jesus died on

103

the Cross. But if it is proved that he did not die on the Cross nor did he rise from the dead then the whole edifice of Christianity tumbles to the ground.[207]

I was first exposed to their thinking when I was general secretary for the British Society for the Turin Shroud and was curious as to why Ahmadi Muslims were taking an interest in the subject. In the open discussion of a symposium on the Shroud held in London in 1977 the reason was apparent: assertions which had been made by a few observers that the image on the Shroud might be that of a still living person had come to their attention, and this was just the kind of 'proof' which destroyed the Christian idea of Jesus' Crucifixion and Resurrection.

Instead of offering radical reinterpretations, it is perhaps more appropriate for Christians to ask the questions posed by Kenneth Cragg: 'What are we to say of the nature of a God who behaves in this way, or the character of a Christ who permits another – even a Judas – to suffer the consequences of an antagonism his own teaching has aroused against himself?'[208]

Perhaps a more fruitful approach to the emotionally charged discussion of Jesus' death on the cross is to begin with the total Muslim image of Jesus, and ask the important question: what do the Christian and Muslim pictures of Jesus have in common?

CHAPTER SEVEN

The Muslim Jesus

It is often remarked that we cannot write a full biography of Jesus Christ from the material we possess in the New Testament. Critics further state that it is almost impossible to disentangle Gospel fact from interpretation. In *The Quest for the Historical Jesus*, Albert Schweitzer[209] suggested that those who were trying to peel back the layers of the miraculous and mythical elements in the Gospels to discover the real Jesus would be surprised at what they found: a misguided fanatic proclaiming an imminent apocalypse and dying in order to bring it about. We do, however, have a basic outline of data upon which all the Gospels agree: Jesus (the Greek form of the Hebrew name 'Yeshua' or 'Joshua') grew up in a Jewish family in Nazareth in Galilee, probably with several brothers and sisters. His mother was Mary, and her husband Joseph the carpenter. He undoubtedly had the usual religious training of a Jewish boy at home and in the synagogue. He began his ministry in his native Galilee around the age of thirty and was baptised by the popular preacher, John. He became well known as a healer and impressive teacher, and his message centred on the coming of God's Kingdom.

Jesus drew to himself a band of disciples who came from rather ordinary backgrounds. His teaching attracted a noticeable amount of popular attention, and when he went to Jerusalem for the Passover he was hailed as the promised Messiah. He incurred the wrath of the temple authorities by saying they had turned 'God's house' into a 'den of thieves'. He was arrested as a troublemaker, and handed over to the Roman authorities. Pilate found him guilty, and he was crucified outside the walls of the city.

The last episode of the Gospel story is the one upon which the foundation of Christianity rests: his Resurrection. His disciples were utterly convinced of his triumph over death, and the growth of the early Church was fired by this event. The bare facts leave any observer perplexed and unmoved. With the addition of Jesus' remarkable insights into human nature, the extraordinary impact of his parables and dealings with the outcasts of society, the pathos of his last days, and his total self-giving, we enter a tradition which has inalterably affected Western civilisation.

The Jesus of *The Gospel of Barnabas* is on many occasions similar to that of the canonical Gospels because, of course, the former book depends on material contained in the latter. There is, however, a pronounced difference as the gospel unfolds: from the outset, Jesus is anxious not to be thought of as divine. In the first miracle recorded in *Barnabas* a leper asks, 'Lord, give me health.' Jesus reproved him, saying: 'Thou art foolish; pray to God who created thee, and he will give thee health; for I am a man, as thou art.' In many instances the compassionate Jesus of the Gospels becomes a rather wooden figure in *Barnabas*, the overall impression being that of an austere personality determined that none should misunderstand the purpose of his ministry, which is to lay the ground for one greater than he. One of the Gospels' most tender and poetic parables, that of the prodigal son, loses its poignancy in *Barnabas* because it is followed by a discussion of the fear of God. The image of Jesus as the Prince of Peace is difficult to find in *Barnabas*: when he talks with Roman soldiers (historically an absurdity), they ask, 'Master, is it lawful to wage war?', to be answered by him, 'Our faith telleth us that our life is a continual warfare upon the earth.'

Barnabas' account of the sermon on the mount is an emasculation of the original, and we also miss the strength of the Gospels' commentary of the difficulty of the rich entering the Kingdom of God. Is this the Muslim Jesus? In a word, no; but Christians reading the Koran are surprised both at the reverence to be found there for Jesus and at the absence from it of any New Testament accounts of Jesus' teachings, his healing of the lame, blind and leprous, his pricking the conscience of the self-righteous and his concern for society's despised.

It is difficult for the Christian reader of the Koran to discover the Jesus he knows so well from years of Church school instruction and the Gospel lessons of the mass. When I first started reading the Koran, I felt Thomas Carlyle's oft-repeated critique was justified: 'a wearisome, confused jumble, crude, incondite ... Nothing but a sense of duty could carry any European through the Koran.'[210] Much of the difficulty is due to the arrangement of the suras. In spite of the fact that the material of the Koran was collected soon after Muhammad's death, it is almost impossible to arrange it in chronological order. The traditional arranging was done by the length of each chapter. The Koran must be read as intended, as a dramatic disclosure made to the prophet Muhammad, and the Christian reader must both suspend his desire for a chronological accounting of biblical personalities he recognises and be prepared for a new assessment of their roles. Old and New Testament figures are mixed together; some Gospel figures appear and others are conspicuously absent.

In discussing the Jesus of the Koran it is perhaps useful – especially for those unacquainted with that holy book – to analyse two goodly sections which deal with Jesus. Selecting them is not easy because despite the fact that Jesus is mentioned in fifteen suras and ninety-three verses, this is in most cases quite briefly and in relationship with the other prophets. I have chosen one example from a sura revealed at Mecca and named for Jesus' mother, Mary (Maryam) and another from the sura 'The Table', revealed at Medina. The first is as follows:

And you shall recount in the Book the story of Mary: how she left her people and betook herself to a solitary place to the east.

We sent to her Our spirit in the semblance of a full-grown man. And when she saw him she said: 'May the Merciful defend me from you! If you fear the Lord, leave me and go your way.'

'I am the messenger of your Lord,' he replied, 'and have come to give you a holy son.'

'How shall I bear a child,' she answered, 'when I am a virgin, untouched by man?'

'Such is the will of your Lord,' he replied. 'That is no difficult thing for Him. "He shall be a sign to mankind," says the Lord, "and a blessing from Ourself. This is Our decree." '

Thereupon she conceived him, and retired to a far-off place. And when she felt the throes of childbirth she lay down by the trunk of a palm-tree, crying: 'Oh, would that I had died and passed into oblivion!'

But a voice below cried out to her: 'Do not despair. Your Lord has provided a brook that runs at your feet, and if you shake the trunk of this palm-tree it will drop fresh ripe dates in your lap. Therefore rejoice. Eat and drink, and should you meet any mortal say to him: "I have vowed a fast to the Merciful and will not speak with any man today." '

107

Then she took the child to her people, who said to her: 'This is indeed a strange thing! Sister of Aaron, your father was never a whore-monger, nor was your mother a harlot.'

She made a sign to them, pointing to the child. But they replied: 'How can we speak with a babe in the cradle?'

Whereupon he spoke and said: 'I am the servant of Allah. He has given me the Gospel and ordained me a prophet. His blessing is upon me wherever I go, and He has commanded me to be steadfast in prayer and to give alms to the poor as I shall live. He has exhorted me to honour my mother and has purged me of vanity and wickedness. I was blessed on the day I was born, and blessed I shall be on the day of my death; and may peace be upon me on the day when I shall be raised to life.'

Such was Jesus, the son of Mary. That is the whole truth, which they are unwilling to accept. Allah forbid that He Himself should beget a son! When He decrees a thing He need only say: 'Be,' and it is.

Allah is my Lord and your Lord: therefore serve Him. That is the right path.

Yet the Sects are divided concerning Jesus. But when the fateful day arrives, woe to the unbelievers! Their sight and hearing shall be sharpened on the day when they appear before Us. Truly, the unbelievers are in the grossest error.[211]

The beginning of this excerpt is reminiscent of the account of the annunciation in the first chapter of Luke – even to Mary's question of Gabriel: 'How can this be ... when I have no husband?' The koranic version, however, is more pointed: 'I am a virgin – Christians are surprised at how strongly the notion of the virgin birth is upheld. The conception of Jesus was the result of a creative decree by God. In the sura 'The Imrans' it says: 'Jesus is like Adam in the sight of Allah. He created him of dust and then he said to him: "Be," and he was.' This is alluded to above. Jesus and Adam were the only men in history created without natural fathers. Joseph is never mentioned in the Koran, but the name 'Mary' occurs more often than in the entire New Testament. However, as Geoffrey Parrinder has pointed out, twenty-three of the thirty-four occasions occur in the title 'Son of Mary'. Some Roman Catholic writers have enthusiastically accepted this reverence, and one, P. Hayek, has written that except for the Roman Catholic doctrine of Mary as the Mother of God, 'all the other dogmas defined by the Church or transmitted by its traditions of worship find a support in the

108

Kur'an, rather weak it is true, but certainly real: the Immaculate Conception, the Presentation in the Temple, the Annunciation, the Virgin Birth, Christmas, and even the Assumption'.[212] Needless to say, no Muslim commentator would accept that assessment.

R. C. Zaehner has suggested that the Muslim attitude towards Christ is 'the exact reverse of that of the rationalists: for they accept all that is miraculous and "absurd", the Virgin Birth, the miracles, and the Ascension, but deny, out of their very veneration for Jesus, the one fact that is admitted by all historians to be authentic, the Crucifixion.'[213]

As noted earlier, there are elements concerning Jesus' infancy which are unique to the Koran and apocryphal gospel material. After feeling 'the throes of childbirth' (which is contradicted in *Barnabas*), Mary 'lay down by the trunk of a palm-tree' and cried. A miraculous brook and fruit from the tree are provided. In the Arabic Infancy Gospel there is an account where mother and child are in a 'desert country' (most likely Egypt, from what follows):[214] 'And in Matarea the Lord Jesus caused a well to spring forth, in which the lady Mary washed his shirt.' The following account in the Gospel of Pseudo-Matthew is strikingly similar to that in the Koran:

On the third day Mary saw a palm and wished to rest under it. When she was seated there she saw fruit on it, and said to Joseph that she should like to have some. Joseph said he was surprised she should say that because the tree was so high: he himself was thinking more about water, of which they had very little left. Jesus sitting in Mary's lap with a joyful countenance bade the palm give his mother of its fruit. The tree bent as low as her feet and she gathered what she would. He bade it rise again, and give them of the water concealed below its roots. A spring came forth and all rejoiced and drank of it.[215]

Mary's 'people' refer to her as 'Sister of Aaron', which is said by commentators to indicate 'a virtuous woman' since in the Koran Aaron is held to be a prophet and saintly man. A claim has been made by Western scholars that Muhammad confused Aaron's sister Miriam with Mary (Maryam), Jesus' mother. Seemingly the only apocryphal parallel for the koranic belief that Jesus spoke from the cradle is in the Arabic Infancy Gospel: 'Jesus spake even when he was in the cradle, and said to his mother: "Mary, I am Jesus the Son of God, that word which thou didst bring forth according to the declaration of the angel Gabriel to thee, and my father hath sent me for the salvation of the world.'[216]

Similarly, in the koranic excerpt quoted previously, Jesus speaks to Mary's 'people', who are surprised at this 'strange thing' – a birth without a natural father. A concise summary of the koranic idea of the son of Mary follows: he is 'the servant of Allah'; has been given the Gospel (*Injil*) and has been ordained a prophet by God. 'Such was Jesus, the son of Mary' continues the sura, adding strongly that he is not Allah's son, as the Arabic Infancy Gospel and some of 'the Sects' maintain.

The title 'Servant of God', as Geoffrey Parrinder writes, 'may not appear remarkable yet in the Bible it has associations with the Messiah'.[217] This is especially important in the prophecies from the Book of Isaiah, and Christians have developed an important identification of Jesus the Messiah with Isaiah's 'Suffering Servant' who was 'wounded for our transgressions ... bruised for our iniquities'.

Obviously none of this connection is intended in the Koran, and the title 'Messiah' (Al-Masih) has no special theological significance for Muslims. As Anawati writes: 'The uncompromising dogma of the unity of God removes any Christian overtones from the word Messiah ... Jesus the Messiah in the Kur'an is only one in a series of prophets which ends with Muhammad.'[218]

As a prophet (*nabi*), Jesus in the Koran is in the succession of the great Hebrew prophets and patriarchs; and in the lists, which number twenty-eight in all, only Jesus and Abraham appear on all occasions. *The Prophets* presents the eight most important: Adam, Noah, Abraham, Joseph, Moses, David, Solomon and Jesus. All have equal reverential treatment, and the author admonishes 'Muslim parents and teachers' to instruct the young about 'certain individuals' chosen by Allah and called prophets 'who tried their best to keep men and women on the right path ... we have not told the story of [the] last Prophet's [Muhammad] life because we think his life should be told in a separate book.'[219] Geza Vermes in his admirable volume *Jesus the Jew*[220] places great stress on the epithet 'prophet' for Jesus; and Oscar Cullman in *Christology of the New Testament* proposes that the title 'prophet' has the advantage of showing the relationship of Jesus to the prophets of the Old Testament: it avoids the political associations of the title 'Messiah'.[221]

In the speech from the cradle, Jesus says: 'I was blessed on the day I was born, and blessed I shall be on the day of my death.' The latter is one of those verses which seems to contradict Sura 4.156f. about the death of Jesus unless, as it has been suggested, this points to a 'final death before the final Resurrection'. The warning given at the end of the excerpt to the 'unbelievers' also speaks of the final days: 'their sight and hearing shall be sharpened on the [judgement] day.' Commentators have proposed that Muhammad could not have had any clear idea of the Jesus of Christian theology in the confusion presented by the sects, with the Nestorians insisting there were two separate persons in the Incarnate Christ and the Monophysites minimising Jesus' human nature. This is not to mention a host of bizarre Gnostic views which still survived: 'The Sects are divided concerning Jesus ... woe to the unbelievers!' could almost be read as an appropriate 'plague on both your houses'.

The second excerpt I have chosen to demonstrate the general koranic attitude towards Jesus is from the period after the hegira, Muhammad's flight to Medina in AD 622:

One day Allah will gather all the apostles and ask them: 'How were you received?' They will reply: 'We do not know. You alone have knowledge of what is hidden.' Allah will say: 'Jesus, son of Mary, remember the favour I have bestowed on you and your mother: how I strengthened you with the Holy Spirit, so that you preached to men in your cradle and in the prime of manhood; how I instructed you in the Scriptures and in wisdom, in the Torah and in the Gospel; how by My leave you fashioned from clay the likeness of a bird and breathed into it so that, by My leave, it became a living bird; how, by My leave, you healed the blind man and the leper, and by my leave restored the dead to life; how I protected you from the Israelites when you brought them veritable signs: when the unbelievers among them said: "This is nothing but plain magic"; how I enjoined the disciples to believe in Me and in My apostle they replied: "We believe; bear witness that we may submit to You utterly." '

'Jesus, son of Mary,' said the disciples, 'can Allah send to us from heaven a table spread with food?'

He replied: 'Have fear of Allah, if you are true believers.'

'We wish to eat of it,' they said, 'so that we may reassure our hearts and know that what you said to us is true, and that we may be witnesses of it.'

'Lord,' said Jesus, the son of Mary, 'send to us from heaven a table spread with food, that it may mark a feast for us and for

111

those that will come after us: a sign from You. Give us our sustenance; You are the best Giver.'

Allah replied: 'I am sending one to you. But whoever of you disbelieves hereafter shall be punished as no man has ever been punished.'

Then Allah will say: 'Jesus, son of Mary, did you ever say to mankind: "Worship me and my mother as gods beside Allah?" '

'Glory to You,' he will answer, 'how could I say that to which I have no right? If I had ever said so, You would have surely known it. You know what is in my mind, but I cannot tell what is in Yours. You alone know what is hidden. I spoke to them of nothing except what You bade me. I said: "Serve Allah, my Lord and your Lord." I watched over them whilst living in their midst, and ever since You took me to You. You Yourself have been watching over them.'[222]

In this excerpt we see a number of other titles and roles assigned to Jesus, but again we have less of the type of information upon which to build a 'biography' than we have from the New Testament. The scene is the day of judgement, and Allah has gathered all the apostles (messengers) for an account of how they were received. To Jesus he records the favours bestowed upon him, making it clear, in almost polemical fashion at the end, that no intention was ever given that Jesus and his mother should be accepted as gods.

The expression 'son of Mary' is repeated several times: it is the most usual title for Jesus in the Koran. The Koran's name for Jesus is Isa, and Mingana asserts that it was in use before Muhammad and was probably not coined by him.[223] The name 'Isa' possibly derives from a phonetic change from 'Yeshuthe', Syriac for 'Jesus', which comes from the Hebrew 'Yeshua'. A monastery in southern Syria bore in AD 571 the name Isaniyah ('of the followers of Jesus'). It has been suggested that Isa is really Esau and was learned by Muhammad from Jews who called Jesus this out of hatred; but this notion seems a fanciful one, and basically the name remains a puzzle to scholars.

The metronymic 'son of Mary' (*Ibn Maryam*) occurs twenty-three times in the Koran and only once in the Gospels: 'Is not this the carpenter, the son of Mary?' (Mark 6.3). It is not known why it is used in the Koran, and suggestions that the title links Jesus with other mortals are reading too much into the koranic text. In the Arabic Infancy Gospel the title appears five times, but in addition to the stories from this gospel that are repeated in the Koran there are, according to Geoffrey Parrinder, many others which employ the title 'son of Mary' and which have no counterpart in the Koran.[224] Interestingly, a Manichaean fragment found amid the ruins of the oasis of Turfan (Turkistan) anathematises among others those who 'invoke the Son of Mary as the Son of the Lord' – apparently, the title was also employed by Manichaeans. Parrinder notes that the Koran calls Jesus not only 'son of Mary' but 'Messiah' without question: 'Its chief objection is to the term Son of God, and perhaps Son of Mary is used in preference because Jesus was undoubtedly the Son of Mary.'[225] That is probably as much as one can wisely speculate as to its prominence in the Koran.

The image of Jesus as a healer and miracle worker is strongly conveyed in Sura 5: he has created living birds from clay, healed the blind and lepers, and brought the dead to life. As with the teachings of Jesus, these great works are alluded to in the Koran, but no details are given. The allusion is always that the full story is already recorded in the *Injil* (Gospel), which to the Christian reader is odd since the New Testament Gospels are considered so unreliable by many Muslim commentators.

The clay birds story is one of many fanciful and frequently tasteless accounts given of Jesus as a child wonder-worker in the Infancy Gospel of Thomas. The version in the 'Greek A' manuscript is as follows:

When this boy Jesus was five years old he was playing at the ford of a brook ... He made soft clay and fashioned from it twelve sparrows. And it was the sabbath when he did this. And there were also many other children playing with him. Now when a certain Jew saw what Jesus was doing in his play on the sabbath, he at once went and told his father Joseph: 'See, your child is at the brook, and he has taken clay and fashioned twelve birds and has profaned the sabbath.' And when Joseph came to the place and saw [it], he cried out to him, saying: 'Why do you do on the sabbath what ought not to be done?' But Jesus clapped his hands and cried to the sparrows: 'Off with you!' And the sparrows took flight and went away chirping. The Jews were amazed when they saw this, and went away and told their elders what they had seen Jesus do.

There is little doubt that Muhammad learned this tale from Christians in Arabia. Ibn Ishaq writes that the Christians of Najran

113

in south-west Arabia argued in favour of the divinity of Christ from his miracles such as 'making clay birds and breathing into them so that they flew away'.[226]

The well-known story of the 'table from heaven' in Sura 5 is peculiar to the Koran, yet Christian observers have noted a relationship to the Gospels' feeding of the five thousand and the last supper. This, however, seems more a case of Christian reinterpretation, which Muslims rightly find very offensive. Many modern Muslim commentators have rejected the popular and literal 'red table of food' sent down upon two clouds to the waiting disciples. Some interpreters prefer the old image. *The Prophets* makes use of the table as the illustration for its chapter on Isa, and says the disciples did not want 'the new miracle' of the table 'in order to believe in Allah but because it (would) make them realize (Jesus was) speaking the truth'.[227]

The end of the excerpt has the eye-catching question from Allah to Jesus: 'did you ever say to mankind: "Worship me and my mother as gods beside Allah?" ' Western commentators have suggested that Muhammad mistakenly thought the Christian Trinity consisted of the Father, the Son and Mary. It is not known what particular Christian heresy Muhammad encountered which might have led to this impression: possibly that of the Arabian Collyridians, who exalted Mary in earth-mother fashion. All Christians can concur with his defence of monotheism expressed earlier in the sura: 'Assuredly they have disbelieved who say: "God is one of three (or 'the third of three')". There is no God but one God.' The 'Holy Spirit' which in the excerpt 'strengthened' Jesus is not here or elsewhere anything like the Christian idea; Muslim commentators say this spirit was the angel Gabriel, who sanctified Jesus and attended on him constantly.

In Chapter 2 a highly debated question was alluded to, that of whether in Sura 61 Jesus foretold the coming of Muhammad: 'I am sent forth to you by Allah to confirm the Torah already revealed and to give news of an apostle that will come after me whose name is Ahmad.' 'Ahmad' in Arabic is usually translated as 'the praised one', and it has been maintained this is another name for Muhammad. Since the Prophet is mentioned by the name 'Muhammad' only a few times in the Koran, this would not be unusual. It has, understandably, been assumed by Muslims that just as other prophets foretold the coming of Jesus, so he must have foretold the coming of Muhammad. This, of course, is a major point in *The Gospel of Barnabas*. Polemicists have charged that Jesus' promise of the Paraclete (John 16.7-8) is really the promise of Muhammad: 'it is for your good that I am leaving you. If I do not go, your Advocate (Comforter) will not come, whereas if I go, I will send him to you.' According to the polemicists, Christians changed the word from an original *periklutos* ('famous, celebrated') to *parakletos* ('comforter').

Sulayman Shahid Mufassir, a former Baptist minister converted to Islam, writing 'A Post-Christmas Thought' in the Muslim periodical *Impact*, recently returned to the argument: 'what Jesus really said in his own language of Aramaic was nearer in meaning to the similar Greek word 'periclyte' (*periklutos*) ... and that "John" – an unknown writer in the second century of the Christian era – picked up "paraclete" in error.' Another possibility he gives is that

some hasty editor was not satisfied with the expression 'spirit of truth' (John 15.26): 'But when your Advocate has come, whom I will send you from the Father – the Spirit of truth' or did not understand it and assumed that this must be the same as the 'Holy Spirit'. The words at John 14.26 which identify the Paraclete as the Holy Spirit are the result of this ('... but your Advocate, the Holy Spirit whom the Father will send in my name ...'). Such words are found nowhere else and are obviously an addition to the text. Yet this premature interpretation, unsound textually, is the one generally accepted by the Church for explaining who the 'Paraclete' is!

Sulayman Mufassir insists that John the evangelist understands the 'Paraclete' to be a flesh-and-blood person, and that 'there is no one else in all of history that John 14.16 *et seq.* could refer to but Muhammad'.[228]

W. Montgomery Watt thinks the term 'Ahmad' should be taken in the sense of an adjective rather than that of a noun,[229] and J. Schacht feels there are strong grounds to believe that the identification of Ahmad with Muhammad 'was not commonly accepted by Muslims until the first half of the second (Muslim) century'.[230]

Even more disputatious is the link of Jesus with the idea of the Mahdi. On 20 November 1979, in Mecca's sacred mosque as 50,000 worshippers celebrated the beginning of Islam's fifteenth century, the dawn prayers were interrupted by a group of 350 armed men and their followers from a nomadic tribe. They demanded that one of their number be declared the Mahdi: the promised saviour who would cleanse Islam. According to the tradition, the Mahdi would be joined in Jerusalem by Jesus, and together they would defeat the false Mahdi (*al-Dajjal*, the Antichrist) from Persia. *The Times* of 22 November, reporting from Jeddah, commented on the latter point: 'The niceness of the setting of present events is being remarked on here.'

The concept of the Mahdi is not to be found in the Koran but developed early in different *hadith* (traditions) during the leadership disputes which followed Muhammad's death. The early history of the Mahdi tradition coincided with ideas of the second coming of Jesus, who as Mahdi was to establish the rule of righteousness. As belief in the Mahdi developed, the activities of Jesus' second coming came to be seen as an accessory event to that of the Mahdi. Jesus still living in the body will appear just before the final day in preparation for the coming of the Mahdi, when the world will be purified of sin and unbelief.

Later the idea of the Mahdi became more a utopian notion whose realisation would occur in a dim future, and it was embellished with crude eschatological fables. Mahdi claimants appeared at the beginning of the new Muslim centuries with the intention of restoring the religious purity of Islam. The 'Mad Mahdi' of the Sudan revolted against the Egyptian administration and died shortly after his capture of Khartoum from General Gordon in 1885. One hundred Muslim years later a Mahdi claimant, Muhammad Abdullah al Qahtani, asserting descent from the Prophet, challenged the temporal and spiritual power of the House of Saud by criticising its 'corrupt Westernized ways'. The capture of Islam's Holy of Holies sent a shock wave throughout the Muslim world, and 9 January 1980 sixty-three of the rebels were publicly beheaded in a number of Saudi towns, including Mecca. The Mahdi claimant had been shot earlier in the fighting when the mosque was retaken by Saudi forces.

Anawati's article on Isa presents the mass of detail which has developed on the tradition of the second coming of Jesus in the following manner:

Jesus, on returning to the earth, will descend on to the white arcade of the eastern gate at Damascus, or, according to another tradition, on to a hill in the Holy Land which is called Afik; he will be clothed in two *musarra*; his head will be anointed. He will have in his hand a spear with which he will kill the Antichrist (al-Dajjal). Then he will go to Jerusalem at the time when the dawn

116

prayer is being said, led by the imam. The latter will try to give up his place to him, but Jesus will put him in front of him and will pray behind the imam following the prescription of Muhammad. Then he will kill all the pigs, will break the cross, destroy the synagogues and the churches, and will kill all the Christians except those who believe in him. Once he has killed the false Messiah (al-Dajjal), all the Peoples of the Book will believe in him, and there will be only one community – that of Islam. Jesus will make justice to reign. Peace will be so complete that it will extend also to the animals among themselves and to man's relations with the animals. Jesus will remain for forty years and then will die. The Muslims will arrange his funeral and will bury him at Medina, beside Muhammad in a place left vacant between Abu Bakr and Umar.[231]

Another Mahdi claimant at the beginning of the fourteenth Muslim century was the founder of the Ahmadiyya movement in Islam, Mirza Ghulam Ahmad of Qadian in the Punjab. In the 1880s he announced he was the Mahdi and Jesus come again. The latter idea was linked with his discovery that the genuine tomb of Jesus was in Srinagar in Kashmir. As discussed earlier, this assumes that Jesus and Yus-Asaph, a little-known local saint, were the same person. (The scholar of Islam Ignaz Goldziher says the tomb is probably of Buddhist origin.[232]) Mirza Ghulam Ahmad's beliefs contradict both orthodox Muslim and Christian traditions concerning Jesus. Finding Jesus' tomb confirmed his conviction that he had appeared 'in the spirit and power of Jesus in the seventh millenium of the world'. It also rekindled interest in the perennial tradition of Jesus' life in India and fired bitter sectarian controversies among Pakistani Muslims. Legally, the sect has been classified as 'non-Muslim' by Pakistan. Muhammad, as the seal of the prophets and presenter of the final revelation of God, had been challenged by a nineteenth-century visionary: the Ahmadi claims were anathema.

It is difficult to form a clear image of Jesus from the Koran. There is no doubting the respect he receives: his many titles, unusual birth and miracles make him a figure second only to Muhammad. For Christians, however, the koranic picture is a shadowy one, and when the eschatalogical traditions are added Isa seems stern and emotionless, a rather unattractive figure. If it were not for the New Testament Jesus to which the koranic message points, his portrait would inspire little devotion.

117

Geoffrey Parrinder wisely warns: 'By isolating Jesus from the rest of the Qur'an and the Islamic tradition we may arrive at a portrait of Jesus that is not the Jesus Muslims know.'[233] To that I would add the presentation of the Gospels. It is interesting to see in this connection the image presented to Muslim children in *The Prophets*.[234] Each chapter lovingly portrays the great prophets of the Koran in capsule story form. Three-fifths of the chapter on Isa deals with Mary and her infancy plus the infancy of John the Baptist. Jesus' infancy includes the stories of the date tree and the miraculous spring. Jesus speaking from the cradle becomes 'the Child Isa defends his mother'. Jesus' miracles include making birds from clay and the table with food from heaven. Isa does not die on the cross and is taken up according to 'St. Barnabas' writing'. The chapter ends with his return 'to this earth in order to kill Dajjal, the terrible unbeliever. After that he would fight and destroy all evil powers and rule the whole world. Every single man and woman alive after all these wars would become a Muslim.' This little book has been making the rounds of comparative religion classes in Britain, and the Christian observer is quite surprised at the picture of Jesus it gives the young.

Aside from theological considerations, the major reason the Muslim concept of Jesus is so different from the general Christian view of him comes from basic differences in evangelistic style between the two religions. Generally, Islam has a simpler and more precise tradition than that of Christianity. It is a highly practical and workable religion – as its founder intended it to be. Jesus and Muhammad present a fascinating comparison of religious figures, although it has been suggested by certain Christian thinkers that theologically it is more appropriate to compare Jesus to the Koran. As Professor Nasr writes: 'In Islam the will of God is revealed in the Qur'an, while in Jesus Christ we have the revelation of God himself.'[235]

Compared to Jesus – or the Buddha – Muhammad appears more a political and social leader than a spiritual prototype. The general Western image of the Buddha is a contemplative figure under the Bo tree; that of Jesus is a compassionate shepherd; and Muhammad is viewed as a rider on horseback brandishing a sword. Nasr has suggested, 'The Prophet should be compared to the prophet kings of the Old Testament, to David and Solomon.' This type of figure, he continues, is 'at once a spiritual being and a leader of men, and has always been, relatively speaking, rare in the Christian West, especially in modern times'.[236] The religious sentiment Christians give to Jesus has no real counterpart in Islam – can one imagine 'Muhammad, Lover of My Soul, Let Me to Thy Bosom Fly', 'What a Friend We Have in Muhammad', 'Muhammad Prophet Superstar'?

In a secular sense, Muhammad's life is a considerable success story: the self-made, illiterate camel-driver who on the strength of a book founded an empire which once stretched from Uzbekistan to France. A book published several years ago in the United States ranked the 'one hundred most influential persons in history' and placed Muhammad in the first position, followed by Sir Isaac Newton and Jesus; next came Buddha, Confucius and St. Paul. The list created a popular fuss. The author, Michael Hart, defended his choice of Muhammad: 'It is his unparalleled combination of secular and religious influence (down to the present day) which I feel entitles Mohammed to be considered the most influential single figure in human history.'[237]

On many points, the known biography of Muhammad of Mecca could not be more opposite to that of Jesus of Nazareth. Born into an influential tribe, Muhammad was married at twenty-five to a woman fifteen years his senior. According to Gospel accounts, Jesus was born in a stable; he grew up in the household of a carpenter from Galilee, and never married. Both began their ministries fairly late in life: Jesus at thirty Muhammad at forty.

Jesus collected a group of fishermen to begin the itinerant preaching of a rather abstract 'Kingdom of God' in his native province. Muhammad became a political and military leader of consummate skill by welding together a force which united the many tribes of Arabia; he took part in some of the early battles, was wounded on one occasion and was known to have killed at least one adversary. Following initial difficulties in his home town, he knew nothing but success, while Jesus turned his ministry to the capital and was arrested, flogged and crucified as a blasphemer and enemy of the state. Rich in years and accomplishments, Muhammad died a natural death while planning a military expedition to the Syrian border in AD 632.

Both men were visionaries, but Muhammad, unlike Jesus, was an extremely practical character. His design for a new religion and world order could not help but succeed; it was explicit and systematic. The Prophet's followers knew exactly what was expected of them: five pillars of faith and a holy book which refined and completed the message of God's prophets culminating in Jesus.

Recently a book presenting 'a Muslim and a Christian in

dialogue' was published in Kenya and the United States. At that time, both its authors were on the faculty of the University of Nairobi. It is to be commended for its candid and thorough approach. After investigating the complicated and divisive viewings of Jesus, the Muslim writer Badru Kateregga, says: 'Muslims have great respect and love for Jesus the Messiah. He is one of the greatest prophets of Allah. To deny the prophethood of Jesus is to deny Islam.' Kateregga goes on to challenge Christian readers: 'The gulf between Christians and Muslims is ... widened by the Christian silence on and non-recognition of Muhammad as the Seal of Prophets, and the final guidance (the Qur'an) that was revealed to him by God.[238] Perhaps it is impossible to give the answers Muslims would like to hear without doing violence to the orthodox Christian message. It is this dialogue, so rich in potential and yet so floundering in direction, which will be our last exploration.

CHAPTER EIGHT

Can We Ever Get Together?

The Economist, 25 December 1982, asks: 'Why study a religion which yours has overtaken? What can you gain especially when the Koran already tells you what Christianity is, and the Christians have plainly got it wrong?'[239]

To indicate the relation between Christian and Muslim beliefs, Alfred Guillaume goes through the Apostles' Creed indicating points with which it and the Koran agree. Undoubtedly some observers will disagree with one or two of his judgements – the words in italics are those rejected by Islam:

I believe in God
the Father
Almighty, Maker of heaven and earth:
And in Jesus Christ
His only Son, our Lord,
Who was conceived by the Holy Ghost, Born of the Virgin Mary,
Suffered under Pontius Pilate, Was crucified
Dead? *and buried, He descended into hell; the third day*
He rose again from the dead,
He ascended into heaven,
And sitteth on the right hand of God the Father Almighty;
From thence He shall come
to judge the quick and the dead.
I believe in the Holy Ghost; [if interpreted as the angel
    Gabriel – my note]
The Holy Catholic Church;
The Communion of Saints;

The Forgiveness of sins;
The Resurrection of the body, And the life everlasting.[240]

When presented in this manner, koranic doctrine agrees with half
of Western Christendom's most popular credal statement. If one
attempted the same with Judaism, the result would be far less; but the
argument could be made that the strong affinity between the Jewish
and Muslim traditions on an uncompromising monotheism
overrides this type of exercise. Be that as it may, one would not
think there was so much possible concurrence between Christians
and Muslims when the antipathy that has existed for centuries is
surveyed. Albert Hourani's *Europe and the Middle East*, which is
based in part on lectures he has delivered at Oxford, gives a
thorough history of the antagonisms:

> It is easy to see the historical relationship of Christians and
> Muslims in terms of holy war, of Crusade and *Jihad*, and there is
> some historical justification for this. The first great Muslim
> expansion in Christian lands, Syria, Egypt and North Africa,
> Spain and Sicily; the first Christian reconquests, in Spain, Sicily
> and the Holy Land; the spread of Ottoman power in Asia Minor
> and the Balkans; and then the spread of European power in the
> last two centuries: all these processes have created and
> maintained an attitude of suspicion and hostility on both sides
> and still provide, if not a reason for enmity, at least a language in
> which it can express itself.[241]

In the earlier days of confrontation, Christians viewed Islam as a
mixture of desert fanaticism, superstition and unchecked sensuality.
The idea of accepting Muhammad as an authentic prophet in the
Judaeo-Christian tradition was impossible. He was, in the eyes of
many Christian polemicists, a charlatan, a warmonger and a
womaniser. The most direct polemical confrontation occurred with
the missionary expansionism which accompanied the overseas
imperialism following the Napoleonic wars.

Generally, for a thousand years Islam had known little but
success and expansion; then the tide turned. Mogul India fell to the
West, and within the century beginning in 1830 the whole of
Muslim North Africa became a European domain. Following
World War I the entire Ottoman empire (under the caliph, a
successor to Muhammad) was dismantled; even Mecca was
effectively under British control. The geographic crescent of Islam

was in the hands of the Christian West and, in the eyes of expansionists, ripe for conversion. A considerable missionary conquest was attempted by a variety of well-meaning and Bible-clutching souls. An example of one of the tracts presented to the home front takes us into the polemical approach of those missionaries. A colleague at the American School in London came across a tract entitled *Mohammedanism: What Is It?*[242] which was published early this century by the 'Fellowship of Faith for the Muslims'. To begin with, the title is insulting to Muslims: it took a long time for Christians to realise that Islam, unlike their own faith and Buddhism was not to be called by its founder's name. The fellowship existed 'to unite in prayer, service, and sacrifice all who love the Moslems, and seek in any way, anywhere, to win them for the Saviour'. In question and answer form those who supported the movement were enlightened as to the work of the missionary.

A number of questions deal with the character of Muhammad and stress his violent nature. When putting forth his prophetic claims 'he had begun to manifest hatred to those whom he considered his enemies ... those whom he opposed were by his orders ruthlessly slain'.

Questions are asked: 'In what great battle was the Moslem invasion of Europe turned back?' (Answer: 'Tours AD 732') and 'Is this to be regarded as an interpretation of Providence?' (Answer 'Most certainly, for up to that point European Christianity was in danger of extinction').

Other questions include the following: 'What outstanding illustrations are there of the triumphs of Islam over Christianity?' Answer: 'The great cathedral of S. Sophia in the capital of the first Christian Emperor of Rome, became a Mohammedan mosque, as did the cathedral of Damascus; Antioch, where the disciples were first called Christians, now "bristles with minarets"; and the Moslem "call to prayer is heard daily in the birth-place of our Lord."'

'What do Moslems mean when they declare that God is merciful?' Answer: 'They usually mean that He will be lenient to the sins of Moslems.'

'Is [the doctrine of Predestination] an essential part of Islam?' Answer: 'It is; for the Moslem true religion is *Islam*, or resignation to the caprice of a divine decree from which there is no escape. The Moslem is nearly always a fatalist, the word *maktoob* (meaning literally "written" or "decreed") being very frequently on his lips.'

'Are there ... spiritual dangers arising from Islamic ritual and practice)' Answer: 'Yes the pomp and ceremony of Islamic ritual and practice appeal to the religious instinct and act as an opiate to the conscience, but exercise no check upon the indulgence of the flesh.'

'Is controversy unavoidable in preaching the Gospel to Moslems? Answer: 'Yes; sooner or later the Christian preacher will be involved in controversy, without seeking it.'

'What should be the attitude of the missionary in regard to controversy?' Answer: 'He should *never seek* it for its own sake, but he should never *shun* it, lest his hearers imagine that no answer can be given to their objections.'

And lastly: 'Is it wise to attack the memory of Mohammad?' Answer: 'No. There is nothing which so readily provokes a fanatical outburst on the part of the hearers.'[243]

It is estimated that after three centuries of proselytising in this manner only a few thousand Muslim souls were 'won for Christ'. Unlike animistic tribesmen, Muslims were not easily converted to another faith. One reason remains to this day: Muslims who abandon their faith are automatically sentenced to death in Islamic countries where the shariah (Islamic law) is enforced.[244]

The tide has turned again for the world's Muslims in the last two decades. With the good fortune and new power brought by oil wealth, a new confidence prevails. It has been suggested that Islam today has the appearance of Christianity a century ago when it renewed its missionary enterprise. According to an *Economist* report, Islam is displaying 'all the signs of flourishing, self-confident missionary health, just as Christianity did'; but interestingly the article goes on to remind us that for the latter that was 'at the very moment when its spiritual roots were being cut away'.[245] That is a salient point: Islam in its 'revival' has not faced – and seems unlikely to face in the foreseeable future – the traumas presented to Christians by Darwinian or Freudian philosophy and the application of critical analysis to its holy book.

After the second 'Islamic summit' of 1973, Colonel Muammar el-Qaddafi declared: 'What we have just accomplished thanks to petroleum is a gift of Allah.'[246] Oil wealth to modern Islam has become what the great conquests of the seventh and eighth centuries were to the Muslims: proof of God's favour. Boastings such as Qaddafi's are expressions of youthful vigour – a fact often forgotten in the West. Of the world's so-called 'great religions' Islam is the youngest. Hinduism and Buddhism are far more ancient, and the former remains limited to India in influence; the

124

latter placid and timeless in the Far East. Islam is roughly 1,300–1,400 years old. It is perhaps beneficial to recollect the condition of Christendom at a similar junction, what it was like circa 1500.[247] The single most important socio-political force in Europe up to the Reformation was, of course, the Holy Catholic Church. Seeds of questioning which led to the Protestant revolution were sown in no small part by Renaissance thought. John Huss was burned for heresy by the Council of Constance, 1414–17; and later Gutenberg's printing press made the Bible available to larger numbers of Christians. Exploration by the Spanish, Portuguese and English opened up a new world for conversion. The Church maintained a tight control of its adherents in Europe: the Council of Constance ended the papal schism and the Inquisition was busy keeping heretical troublemakers in line. In 1453 Constantinople fell to the Ottoman Turks, but following this trauma and the return of Spain to Catholic power the two religions began to resign themselves to boundaries of influence which basically remain to this day.[248]

Islam's present-day renaissance has not incorporated the secular and humanist influences which pervaded that of the fourteenth and fifteenth centuries in Europe. The likelihood of that type of movement in the Islamic world today is even dimmer than the possibility of a Protestant-style rebellion. The present-day Muslim revival is one of closing ranks and hardening the theological shell. V. S. Naipaul, in *Among the Believers*, has a Pakistani teacher of theology saying: 'Khomeini is a good man. He is Islamic ... He has banned women from appearing on television.' Naipaul comments, 'That was all he knew of Iran since the revolution.'[249] The process of Islamisation in many Muslim quarters is mainly a return to puritanism – reinstating the purdah for women, and prohibiting pornographic literature, pop music and the sale of alcohol.[250]

Outside their circles no one went as far as Muhammad in meeting Christians half-way. As we have seen, Jesus is *the* prophet before Muhammad and Messiah. For Christians there is no corresponding acceptance of Muhammad; he has no position in Christian theology. In a sense, this is odd. As Albert Hourani writes, '[Islam] is *the* prophetic religion *par excellence*; and even Christians when they speak of *the* Prophet usually mean Muhammad'.[251] Muslims find the absence of Christian and Jewish recognition of Muhammad's prophethood a basic insult to their faith – as, indeed, did Muhammad himself. After all, the Prophet is clearly entrenched in the Judaeo-Christian tradition: he is the seal of a great line of prophets who re-established the pure faith once

125

delivered to father Abraham. Muslim apologetics emphasise this point. Muhammad made clear a message obscured and corrupted in the Jewish and Christian religions – but what Christians and Jews want to admit to that indictment? As Hourani says, 'the mere fact that Muhammad appeared after Christ is no argument that his revelation was not a true revelation.'[252]

For orthodox Christians, there can be no new revelation after the Incarnation of the God's Son. Jesus is God made man – what point would there be in the sending of a new prophet after that? What more could God do than send his own Son to die for man's sins? The same reaction has been given by Christians to other new prophets who sought to perfect the revelation in Jesus, Mani and the Mormons' Joseph Smith among others.[253] Orthodox Muslims should be reminded they have given the same reaction to the founder of the Ahmadiyya movement in Islam.

The dearth of Judaeo-Christian acceptance of Muhammad has, however, had no effect on the remarkable increase in conversions Islam has gained in the past two decades. Muslim spokesmen speak confidently of having a thousand million adherents by the turn of the twenty-first Christian century. It has been claimed that in Black Africa (south of the Sahara) where Christian and Muslim missionaries are in competition, Islam gains ten converts for every one who accepts the Christian faith. A 1980 German Catholic publication, *Islam in Black Africa*, gave wide evidence of this growing strength and drew attention to the fact that 'Religion and politics are ... so united and mixed that we can say that any religious advance of Islam in a country is at the same time a political advance, and vice versa that any political advance is a religious advance.'[254] Some Catholic publications show a great admiration for this aspect of Islam – like a wistful remembrance of former days. A Catholic Truth Society publication dealing with Muslims in Britain says: 'One of the great strengths of Islam lies in the fact that it is not only a religion but a community; a culture, a civilisation – *umma*.'[255] No Christian group better understands the full import of Islam than does Roman Catholicism. In the final section of the pamphlet, there is the recognition that 'Both religions are expansionist: the Catholic Church through mission, Islam through *dawa*, or calling.' The propagation of Islam to all people is a religious duty for each Muslim, his calling. Until fairly recent times, there was no organised missionary activity by Islam: every Muslim was considered a missionary. In the past few decades, Muslims have taken an interest in Christian-style techniques of missionary work.

126

The Ahmadiyya movement led the way, and their literature has the flavour of old-style Christian missionary tracts. Such titles are issued as 'Death on the Cross? and True Christianity and How It Leads to Islam.[256] The Ahmadiyya movement launched a nationwide crusade at its 1978 International Symposium on 'The Deliverance of Jesus from the Cross' with its leader, Imam Rafiq, declaring 'Britain was a ripe field for conversion to Islam'. Rafiq explained that the Ahmadis 'felt it was time to bring Europe and America back to a living communion with God ... Christianity had failed to do this.'

There has been a remarkable expansion of Islam in Western Europe in the past fifteen years, due mainly to an influx of foreign workers and immigrants from Pakistan, Turkey and other Islamic countries. In 1945, there was only one mosque in England, by 1976 there were 200. Paris, Vienna and Geneva are among many European centres with mosques, and, most interestingly, there will soon be a new addition: Rome. High on Monte Mario, north of the Vatican, an Islamic centre is being constructed for which Libya has allocated ten million dollars and the Saudi government twenty million. There are now more Muslims than Methodists in Britain, and for every Protestant in France there are now two Muslims. Turkey and Russia apart, there are now approximately ten million Muslims in Western Europe.

Generally, Muslims fare better in non-Muslim states than non-Muslims in Islamic countries. There is not one country with a Christian majority where Muslims do not have full freedom to practise their religion, build mosques and distribute the Koran. Religious freedom is refused Christians and other sects in several Arab countries. The idea of a Christian church being built in Mecca is impossible: non-Muslims are not even allowed in the holy city, and airplanes can not fly over it. In Saudi Arabia there are more than 100,000 Catholic foreigners, but no priest or church is tolerated. The restrictions imposed upon any sort of Christian missionary work in Muslim lands or the distribution of bibles is well publicised. Bahai's in Iran and Ahmadis in Pakistan have been actively persecuted.[257]

G. H. Jansen makes a good point in this respect:

If nothing can be done to change the fundamental inferiority of non-ideological minorities in an ideological state, the Muslim world – now more than ever interested in itself – has discovered a fact about itself that could mitigate such crudities as Khomeini's idea of a poll tax on non-Muslims. This fact is that around one quarter of the world's 750 million Muslims are minorities in non-Muslim countries ... Sheer self-interest, the *quid pro quo*, would indicate that the Islamic state should deal at least justly with its non-Muslims if it expects similar treatment for its own co-religionist minorities.[258]

As Jansen further reminds Muslims, Islam has had an admirable past record of fair treatment of non-Muslims in many lands. The current lack of reciprocity is a major reason why the Christian-Muslim dialogue flounders; granted, the unsavoury memory of Christian missionary activity still smarts in many areas of the Muslim world, and the actions of Christian fundamentalist sects in Muslim domains are often deplorable. *The Minaret* magazine refers to one of the first encounters between Muslim students and their Christian opposite numbers in London where, after a heated discussion, one Muslim speaker said: 'Christian missionaries in Muslim countries should pack their bags and return home. Otherwise they may be forced to leave the countries by governments of the lands. If governments do not act soon, the public may take the law into their own hands'. The article goes on to say that after many meetings and discussions between members of both religions 'many Muslims who take part in these discussions feel that the Christians have not yet put their cards on the table in spite of the clear stand of the Qur'an demonstrated by Muslims in different ways'. Especially disliked are the attempts to make Christians out of Muslim immigrants in Britain. The article is rather vague about specifically by whom and how this has been happening, but adds: 'Various branches of the host community arrange welcoming parties and social clubs of all descriptions [for the Muslim immigrants]. Although the charitable attitude of the host community is appreciated one gets the feeling of certain hidden motives behind it.'[259]

Stephen Hugh-Jones in *The Economist* puts a number of 'cards on the table' in discussing the Muslim-Christian dialogue:

There *is* Christian-Moslem dialogue, there is readiness to collaborate on practical issues, especially in Europe, there is a sense of common front against a secular world ... But theologically there is no meeting of minds, and those rare Moslem-Christian gatherings that have tried to wander on to doctrinal ground have run into a brick wall. 'We've learned better than to try,' says one Christian participant.

128

The imbalance of approach between a world still confident of its faith, and one that used to be but is no longer, one that joins God with Caesar and one that separates them, explains many features of the Moslem world that westerners find irritating.

Why, for instance, is Christian mission wrong, but Moslem mission, *dawa*, all right? At one level the Moslem answer is 'Because you try to convert *us*, while we only aim at pagans.' Even if this were so, at another level the answer is that which any Victorian evangelist might have given – we are preaching truth and you are preaching error.

Why is the voluntary conversion theoretically permitted in Moslem countries in practice a one-way street? Not only because of social pressures but because apostasy from Islam is, in Moslem tradition, albeit not current practice, an offence against not just the faith but the state (indeed 'political treason' deserving 'banishment, life imprisonment or capital punishment', to quote not some nineteenth-century polemic but a text-book on his faith today written by a perfectly serious Moslem and published three years ago for use in American high schools).'

Why, in Egypt, may a Moslem man marry a Christian woman, but not vice versa? Because, says al-Azhar, Moslems recognise Christianity but Christians do not recognise Islam; so you can be sure a Moslem husband will treat his wife rightly, but not the other way about.'[260]

Intermarriage between Muslims and Christians has become a concern in European countries. The Centre Jean-Bart in Paris issued a report earlier this year which declared that in France nine out of ten such unions are destined to failure. Among the difficulties the authors mentioned was 'according to the Koran each child of a mixed marriage is a Muslim automatically at birth, and in the event of a divorce – which may be pronounced unilaterally by the husband – a non-Muslim wife has no right to custody of her children: this, in particular, has led to the collapse of many marriages'.[261]

Despite such difficulties, Islam continues to better its condition in Western Europe. Six hundred imams and mosque administrators at a conference at Wembley in April 1984 established a council of 'elders' to represent Britain's 1.8 million Muslims. The body will operate similarly to the Jewish Board of Deputies, handling the special problems and concerns of a religious minority. It is believed to be the first such initiative taken in a non-Muslim country and

129

will undoubtedly set the pattern for other European Muslim communities. It certainly marks a coming of age of Islam in Western Europe.

There are a number of institutions in Britain which aim at bettering relations between Christians and Muslims. The Islamic Council and Islamic Foundation in Leicester publish attractive pamphlets directed at Christians, drawing attention to beliefs held in common by the two religions. Selly Oak College in Birmingham has a centre for the study of Islam and Christian-Muslim relations offering degrees in Islamic studies; and its international summer school includes Muslim and Christian leaders, teachers and students from a number of countries. The Birmingham centre has worked hard to pinpoint difficulties Muslims in Britain have in adjusting to their new environment: Muslim religious education for the young, and the reticence of some officials to grant space and permission for the building of mosques and Islamic centres.

The first official effort to define a Christian attitude towards Islam came with the Second Vatican Council's document *Nostra Aetate*. Although, as Albert Hourani reminds us, the statement does not deal with the status of Muhammad or of the Koran, in a historical sense it marks a dramatic change of attitude by the largest segment of Christendom:

> Upon the Muslims, too, the Church looks with esteem. They adore one God, living and enduring, merciful and all-powerful, Maker of heaven and earth and Speaker to men. They strive to submit whole-heartedly even to His inscrutable decrees, just as Abraham, with whom the Islamic faith is pleased to associate itself. Though they do not acknowledge Jesus as God, they revere Him as a prophet. They also honour Mary, His virgin mother; at times they call on her, too, with devotion. In addition, they wait the day of judgment when God will give each man his due after raising him up. Consequently, they prize the moral life, and give worship to God especially through prayer, almsgiving, and fasting.
>
> Although in the course of the centuries many quarrels and hostilities have arisen between Christians and Muslims, this most sacred Synod urges all to forget the past and to strive sincerely for mutual understanding.[262]

There have been a number of ecumenical gatherings between Christians and Muslims since this statement was issued. A number of prestigious conferences of scholars from both religions have been sponsored by the Vatican's Secretariat for Non-Christians, the World Council of Churches and the Vatican's admirable Centre of Studies for Muslim-Christian Dialogue which publishes the useful *Islamochristiana*. Some of these meetings have been marked by bitter exchanges, and a number of participants think it better to concentrate on the practical, everyday level of problems and concerns. Perhaps several more decades will have to pass before serious theological differences can be more frankly and less emotionally debated. Several spokesmen seem ready for more. Egyptian scholar Abdel aziz Kamel asked at the 1977 Muslim-Christian Congress of Cordoba: 'Does dialogue mean merely polite conversation and diplomacy? Must not questions be raised in all honesty and charity if we want to progress together in dialogue?'[263] The Jesuit Victor Mertens, who has worked in Zaïre for many years, feels that dialogue 'must be lucid and must avoid any trace of naiveté by overidealising the situation'. He also asks 'whether so far we have not been too timid in our attitude toward certain Muslims.'[264]

The Christian-Muslim dialogue held in April 1982 at Colombo under the joint auspices of the World Council of Churches and the World Muslim Congress made some feasible suggestions: the establishment of a joint standing committee which hopefully would include Roman Catholics and international Islamic organisations other than the World Muslim Congress; co-operation at national and local levels regarding the needs of Christian and Muslim refugees; the recognition of the need to study and safeguard the rights of religious minorities; and the appeal that the role of dialogue should recognise the issue of legitimate evangelism and avoid being a form of proselytism. This was issued in the report of the World Council of Churches delegation.

As previously noted, Jan Slomp is one of the few observers of the Muslim scene actively involved in the process of dialogue who has noted the detrimental use of *The Gospel of Barnabas* in some sections of the Islamic world. Slomp also offers wise advice for the next stages of the dialogue:

Mutual respect is a *conditio sine qua non* (indispensable condition) for dialogue. If we as Christians accept as a point beyond discussion that the Muslims consider the Holy Quran to be the final Word of God and Muhammad as the Prophet, then the least we may expect is that our Muslim partner will respect our

Christian right to affirm what the Church considers to be Holy Scripture and what not. It is unreasonable to expect that Christians will respond positively when they are challenged by the demand: you ought to believe this spurious gospel of Barnabas than the four Gospels which all orthodox Christians everywhere and always have accepted as the final records of God's self-revelation in Christ. The only basis for dialogue is the right of the participants to state what they believe rather than what they according to outsiders ought to believe. To give up such a right would mean a loss of one's identity as Muslim or Christian. When one of the partners loses his identity, dialogue is no longer possible or meaningful.[265]

Those last words of Slomp's could be written in response to a well-meaning attempt to make over the ecumenical partner in another image, a book already quoted, *The Koran in the Light of Christ*. Its author, Basetti-Sani, relates that he originally studied Islam in order 'to destroy an enemy' and ended up discovering an entirely different approach toward the old adversary: 'a Christian interpretation of the Sacred Book of Islam'. Basetti-Sani argues that the,

interpretation which Muslim theology has for centuries given of the Koran's message and Mohammed's mission ... after the first five hundred years of the Hegirah, was primarily the work of Jews and Christians who converted to Islam. Their contribution, it is easy to understand, unfortunately had a strong influence on the anti-Christian orientation which Islam adopted in its historical and doctrinal development. If this is indeed the sole interpretation the Koran may have, I do not see how dialogue between Christians and Muslims can be successfully initiated.

The Franciscan does not veil his feelings, and he proceeds to give the type of interpretation which would be acceptable. His contention that the Christianity Muhammad experienced 'was no longer an authentic Christianity ... he never knew the doctrine of the Catholic Church of orthodox Christianity – hence he was unable to reject it' is beside the point with Muslims today – and unacceptable. There is no likelihood that Muslims will make this admission.

Basetti-Sani goes on:

132

Muslim exegesis has studied the Koran for centuries solely in its aspect of a 'divine' production, and has neglected the human aspect. I think it is the duty of Christian students to help the Muslim place the texts of the Koran back in the living environment in which the texts were born ... It is almost impossible to find points of contact between Christianity and Islam in the traditional Muslim interpretation of the Koran ... Could not I try to see whether the message of the Koran might look quite different when it is viewed in the authentic light of Christian revelation?

The author criticises previous Western koranic analyses indicating Gnostic or Jewish influences on the Koran, and yet 'discovers the (orthodox Christian) Christ in the full meaning of the texts'. He thinks it

a great favour for Muslim exegetes if we could persuade them to (use) the principles of modern criticism which have been so successful ... the Muslim exegete tends to see the 'word of God' as immobile, fixed, absolute ... and once the Koran was taken as 'absolute', Islam became isolated. That is why any research into possible influences upon the formation of the Koran is excluded. The theory that makes the book 'fallen from heaven' prevents the Muslim from discovering through scientific literary criticism, all the cultural, literary, religious, juridical, and social influences which have worked together to form it.[266]

I have given vent to Basetti-Sani's writing because it is such a remarkable example of basic obstacles to future dialogue and yet is presented in an irenic manner. Few Christians have gone this far in trying to meet Muslims on their own terms, and fewer have ended in a more unsatisfactory result. In the final analysis, *The Koran in the Light of Christ* is basically similar to the koranic dissections of former years that present-day Western Islamic scholars attack so vehemently. Basetti-Sani and others of his ilk are offering an interpretation of the Koran not requested by the Muslim partner in dialogue, and one which asks Muslims to see in their holy book interpretations they do not wish to make. There have been many of these well-intentioned 'Christian interpretations' of the Islamic faith and, usually from sheer desire to be fair and 'ecumenical' in approach, they have ended up reading large Christian meanings into Islamic concepts.

133

There is another Christian reading of Islam: one which is difficult to take seriously but fairly popular among fundamentalists. During and following the Iranian take-over of the American embassy there was a proliferation of books on 'militant Islam' with lurid titles like *I Escaped from Islam* and *The Muslim Design of Conquest*.[267] Many of these contained a strongly polemical attack upon Islam. One example, originally published in Germany, has made the rounds in Britain. *The Unholy War* by Marius Baar has in the English version the subtitle 'Oil, Islam and Armageddon'. The back cover tells us that the author

worked among the Moslems for twenty-five years, has researched the Koran and biblical prophecies and reached the frightening conclusion that today's world problems are, in fact, spiritual in nature, and that the triumph of Ayatollah Khomeini is a call to awaken the last world power. Before its final destruction, the people of Israel made a choice between Christ and Barabbas. Baar warns that at the end of time, the nations face yet another choice. Will it be Christ or Mohammed?[268]

As the publisher's foreword says, the book was written by a 'man who takes the Bible seriously' and Baar unfolds a scenario which begins with the biblical figures of Isaac and Ishmael:

Two parallel lines of descent stem from Abraham. One line is that of his 'natural' son Ishmael, born of the maidservant Hagar; he is the ancestor of the Arabs. Abraham's other son, Isaac, the son 'of promise' born of Sarah his wife, is the ancestor of the Jews. Jesus, the Christ promised from the beginning of the Old Testament, is Isaac's descendant. Isaac's line brought salvation into the world, though its final accomplishment is yet to come. This is the lineage of God, the Christian line. Ishmael's descendants include the Amalekites, the Philistines (all hereditary enemies of the Jews) and Mohammed, the founder of Islam. This is the anti-Christian line, and the two sets of descendants have always fought.[269]

And, according to this book, they will continue to fight to the end of time - so much for dialogue. 'Today it is easy to see that the restoration of Israel is a fulfillment of biblical prophecy, since today the state of Israel actually exists.' The restoration of Israel is a signal announcing the 'end times' - nations will be judged on their attitude toward Israel. The nations will be deceived into thinking their security lies with Ishmael, and 'will one by one give up on Israel because of the importance of oil for their economies.' Baar also sees some odd similarities between Islam and 'liberal' Christianity: 'Islamic teachers are doing exactly what some theologians have done. They claim that some of Jesus' statements are false or were added later and other statements, because they agree with their theories are authentic.'[270]

This is a disturbing book in many respects. It is the fundamentalist position most of us prefer to overlook – and in Britain it is easily dismissed. In my native land of America that is not so easily done with the increasing strength of fundamentalist groups. Like most fundamentalists, Baar presents a case which can be neatly and frighteningly (and superficially) fixed into the chaos of our day: 'It is fascinating to see how events are unrolling according to a definite plan. They seem to be synchronized and heading to a climax. Consider the recent changes in the economy, in armaments, and in theology. As with Jewish and Islamic fundamentalists, Jerusalem is *a* if not *the* focal point of the impending drama of the 'end times'.[271]

In many respects Jerusalem is a symbol of all that divides and unites Judaism, Christianity and Islam: all the hate and all the promise. Here the temple will be rebuilt and the true Messiah come at length to lead mankind towards heaven. Here God's son was crucified and rose from the dead. Here the Prophet ascended to heaven into the presence of Allah. The old city of Jerusalem is a constant reminder of the fragmentation and jealousy among Christian groups: Armenians, Catholics, Greeks and Copts all squabbling over their rights to Jesus' sepulchre – a scene Muhammad would well have understood. Jews wail at the crumbling remains of a long-lost temple, and some zealots among them recently attempted to establish a symbolic settlement at the holiest Islamic shrine after Mecca and Medina. Jerusalem is quartered – Christian, Armenian, Jewish and Muslim – and has been made the capital of a state which would go to any lengths to continue control over it. It is a place where frenzied literalisms are acted out daily, where it is difficult for Muslims not to hate Jews and the Christians who side with them. It is where Jews are able to control Muslims, and Christian priests get spat upon by Arab boys. Yet despite it all, it goes on, and at sunset when it is bathed in a golden hue, it is easy to believe it is the holy city.[272]

If Jerusalem can continue to make it – at least in some fashion – then perhaps there is hope that Muslims, Jews and Christians will gradually come to understand one another better and, if not loosen some sectarian boundaries, at least guarantee the rights of each where it is in a minority position. If the fundamentalists of each group have it right – and one always wonders how so many different sects can have such a monopoly on the truth – then we are in trouble.

Fundamentalists appear to be on a collision course. The recent scene of forty-one Jewish militants attempting an occupation of the Temple Mount, followed by armed police and soldiers patrolling the narrow alleyways around the Muslim holy places in Jerusalem, is a reminder of a possible future explosion. The attempt on the Pope's life by a Turkish Muslim though perhaps not for religious reasons sent shivers down Christian spines. One can almost believe Revelation's Armaggedon will be a cataclysmic clash of religious fanatics – with Jerusalem as the likely setting.

Too many attempts at dialogue between Christians and Muslims in the past have been plagued by both sets of religionists reading their own meanings into the other's theological concepts. Both sides are guilty of using offensive propaganda; both are guilty of mistrust and arrogance. Slomp has said:

> the demand that the Christians should believe ... Pseudo-Barnabas rather than the four gospels ... is a failure to take seriously on his own terms the Christian partner in the dialogue which is sorely needed ... If some Muslims consider the purpose of dialogue to be conversion, they are perfectly entitled to do so. Some Christians also see the final purpose of dialogue conversion. Muslims who try to use dialogue as a means of converting Christians better do so on the basis of the Holy Qur'an than on the basis of a medieval forgery.[273]

These things must be said; these cards should be put on the table. Muslims in the freedom of a new society cannot hope to escape critical analysis of their propositions any more than is the case with Christian and Jewish groups in Britain. For better or worse, this has become an established feature of modern Western society. There are many areas in which Islam and Christianity and Judaism are complementary, and at the same time there are significant differences. All three need to learn much more about one another.

There is much to be admired in Islam: Allah is a truly universal God knowing no chosen people, racial discriminations or hint of theological division of unity. Muhammad provided millions with a

136

far better understanding of God and a more civilised society than they had previously. An awareness of the tensions and polemic created by the new mood and vigour of Muslims is essential for Jews and Christians. The three great religions born in the Near East have much in common and also must come to terms with the problems peculiar to religious brothers. The possibility that Muhammad was exposed to an unusual variety of sectarian influences in the revelation of the Koran and the recognition of the untenable character of documents like *The Gospel of Barnabas* in no way detract from the essential Muslim achievement. If anything, such things indicate a more human and apprehensible side of Islam.

Chapter Notes and References

Introduction

1 Slomp, Jan, 'Pseudo-Barnabas in the Context of Muslim-Christian Apologetics', *Al-Mushir* (April, May, June 1974), Christian Study Centre, Rawalpindi.
2 Nichols, Peter, *The Pope's Divisions* (Harmondsworth: Penguin, 1981).
3 Dawood, N. J. (translator), *The Koran* (Harmondsworth: Penguin, 1956).
4 Parrinder, Geoffrey, *Jesus in the Qur'an* (London: Faber, 1965; Sheldon Press, 1976).
5 Hourani, Albert, *Europe and the Middle East* (London: Macmillan, 1980).
6 Grendler, Paul F., *The Roman Inquisition and the Venetian Press 1540-1604* (Princeton, New Jersey: Princeton University Press, 1977).
7 Ragg, Lonsdale and Laura, *The Gospel of Barnabas* (Oxford: Clarendon, 1907). This volume is difficult to come by in libraries. I know of two sources: the British Library and the University Library, Cambridge.

Chapter One

8 This is an abridged account of the story given by George Sale in the introduction to his 1734 translation of the Koran.
9 James, Montague, *The Apocryphal New Testament* (Oxford: Clarendon, 1980; first published 1924).
10 Raggs, *The Gospel of Barnabas*.
11 Gairdner, W. H. Temple, *The Gospel of Barnabas* (Cairo: Church Missionary Society, 1907; reprinted Hyderabad: Henry Martyn Institute of Islamic Studies, 1975).
12 Quoted in Jomier, Jacques, 'L'Evangile selon Barnabé', *Mélanges*, vol. 6 (1959–61), Institut Dominicain d'Etudes Orientales, Cairo.
13 Pines, Shlomo, *The Jewish Christians According to a New Source* (Jerusalem: Hebrew Academy of Sciences and Humanities, 1966).

14 Aguilar, E. Galindo, 'Muslim–Christian Congress of Cordoba (1977)', *Islamochristiana*, 4 (1978), Pontifico Istituto di Studi Arabi, Rome.

15 'Ata ur-Rahim, Muhammad, *Jesus, A Prophet of Islam* (London: MWH, 1979; Karachi: Begum Aisha Bawany Waqf, 1980).

16 Hafizullah, Qazi Muhammad, in foreword to *The Gospel of Barnabas* (Lahore: Al-Kitab, 1981). Except for the added introduction, this is the Raggs's 1907 translation.

17 Ashraf, Syed Ali, *The Prophets* (London: Hodder & Stoughton for the Union of Muslim Organisations, 1980).

18 Enslin, M. S. 'New Testament Apocrypha' in *The Interpreter's Dictionary of the Bible* (New York: Abingdon-Cokesbury, 1976).

19 Grant, Robert, *The Formation of the New Testament* (London: Hutchinson, 1962).

20 Enslin, *The Interpreter's Dictionary*.

21 *The Aquarian Gospel, The Twenty-Ninth Chapter of Acts*, and *The Gospel of Josephus* can all be found in Goodspeed, Edgar J., *Strange New Gospels* (Chicago: University of Chicago Press, 1931).

22 Bock, Janet, *The Jesus Mystery* (Los Angeles: Aura Productions, 1980).

23 Faber-Kaiser, A., *Jesus Died in Kashmir* (London: Sphere, 1978).

24 Goodspeed, *Strange New Gospels*.

25 *The Life of Saint Issa, Best of the Sons of Men* can be found in Bock, *The Jesus Mystery*.

26 Max Müller, Friedrich, quoted in Goodspeed, *Strange New Gospels*.

27 *The Crucifixion of Jesus by an Eye-Witness* can be found in Goodspeed, *Strange New Gospels*.

28 Goodspeed, *Strange New Gospels*.

29 Charfi, Abdelmajid, 'Christianity in the Qur'an Commentary of Tabari', *Islamochristiana*, 6 (1980), Pontifico Istituto di Studi Arabi, Rome.

30 Grant, *The Formation of the New Testament*.

31 Hennecke, Edgar, *New Testament Apocrypha*, vol. 2, Schneemelcher, W. (ed.), (London: Lutterworth, 1965).

32 St. Alban Wells, Leonard, 'The Gospel of Peter', *Hastings Encyclopaedia of Religion and Ethics* (Edinburgh: Clark, 1926).

33 Cirillo, Luigi and Frémaux, Michel, 'Évangile de Barnabé (Paris: Beauchesne, 1977).

34 Pines, *The Jewish Christians*.

35 A good discussion of Jewish Christian groups is to be found in Simon, Marcel, *Jewish Sects at the Time of Jesus*, trans. Farley, James H. (Philadelphia: Fortress, 1967).

36 Blunt, A. W. F., *The Acts of the Apostles (The Clarendon Bible)* (Oxford: Clarendon, 1923).

37 Ibid.

38 Pines, *The Jewish Christians*.

39 Slomp, Jan, 'The Gospel in Dispute', *Islamochristiana*, 4 (1978), Pontifico Istituto di Studi Arabi, Rome.

40 Stern, Samuel, 'Quotations from Apocryphal Gospels in 'Abd Al-Jabbar', *Journal of Theological Studies*, vol. 18 (April 1967), Oxford University Press. In the following issue (April 1968), Stern was highly critical of the paper which Pines had delivered at the Hebrew Academy of Sciences and Humanities. He said that the latter's sensational claim that a 'new source' of information concerning the Jewish Christians of the early centuries had been found 'is based on an erroneous reading of the Text'. The publication was called 'a regrettable act of folly by a distinguished scholar'. We return to the argument in Chapter 4. In my opinion, Jabbar's document is far more interesting in taking us back to early sources of Muslim polemics against such Christian concepts as the Crucifixion; and the tone of debate is remarkably similar to what we experience today.

41 As quoted in *Time* magazine, 15 July 1966.

42 Faruqui, Mumtaz Ahmad, *The Crumbling of the Cross* (Lahore: Ahmadiyya Anjuman Isha'at-i-Islam, 1973).

43 Stern, *Journal of Theological Studies*.

44 Faruqui, *The Crumbling of the Cross*.

45 Raggs, *The Gospel of Barnabas*.

Chapter Two

46 'Ata ur-Rahim, *Jesus, A Prophet of Islam*.

47 Burkitt, F. C., *Acts of the Apostles* (London: Macmillan, 1924).

48 'Ata ur-Rahim, *Jesus, A Prophet of Islam*.

49 Faber-Kaiser, *Jesus Died in Kashmir*.

50 There are a number of Ahmadi tracts dealing with this subject. Most of them are based on the writings of the founder, perhaps best presented in *Jesus in India* (Rabwah:Ahmadiyya Muslim Foreign Missions Department, 1962).

51 Nazir Ahmad, Al-Haj Khwaja, *Jesus in Heaven on Earth* (Lahore: Abeez Manzil, 1972).

52 Ibid.

53 Temple Gairdner, *The Gospel of Barnabas*.

54 *The Koran*, translated with notes by Sale, George (London: Warne, no date).

55 Fletcher, J. E. 'The Spanish Gospel of Barnabas', *Novum Testamentum*, vol. XVIII (1976) Brill, Leiden.

56 de la Monnoye, Bernard, quoted in Raggs, *The Gospel of Barnabas*.

57 John Toland's *Nazarenus* can be read in the British Library, and he seems most impressed by 'his discovery'.

58 Toland, John, quoted in Raggs, *The Gospel of Barnabas*.

59 Slomp, *Islamochristiana*.

60 A fairly long biography is to be found in *Dictionaire de Biographie Chrétienne* (Paris: Aux Ateliers Catholiques du Petit-Montrouge, 1851). There is also a short entry in *Enciclopedia Cattolica* (Vatican City: Libreria Editorce Vaticana, 1953).

61 I would like to thank the Diocese of Fulham and Gibraltar for supplying me with his obituary notices.

62 Raggs, *The Gospel of Barnabas*.

63 Ragg, Lonsdale, 'The Mohammedan "Gospel of Barnabas"', *Journal of Theological Studies*, vol. 6 (1904–5), Oxford University Press.

64 Raggs, *The Gospel of Barnabas*.

65 Slomp, *Islamochristiana*.

66 Raggs, *The Gospel of Barnabas*.

67 Ibid.

68 Ibid.

69 Ibid.

70 Ibid.

71 Al-Kitab, *The Gospel of Barnabas*.

72 Ashraf, *The Prophets*.

73 Anawati, G. C. 'Indjil' in *Encyclopaedia of Islam*, new edition (Leiden: Brill, 1971).

Chapter Three

74 Biruni regarded the four gospels as 'recensions', and mentions 'other gospels in the possession of the Marcionites, the Bardesanites and the Manichaeans'. Given all the differing versions, he considers that 'the prophetic value is not greatly to be trusted ...' The question as to how the material in the Koran dealing with 'Gospel characters and facts' is to be related to the Koran presents no difficulties. 'It is the same God who reveals both books, and the Prophet Muhammad, having received the Revelation directly from God, had no need to consult, directly or indirectly, the Scriptures in order to be able to reproduce some of the features which are found in them.' The foregoing is based on Anawati's article noted above.

75 'Ali, Yusuf, *Commentary on the Qur'an* (Beirut: Dar al Arabia, 1965).

76 Al-Kitab, *The Gospel of Barnabas*.

77 Bowman, John, 'The Debt of Islam to Monophysite Syrian Christianity', *Nederlands Theologisch Tijdschrift*, (1964–5), Veenman and Zonen, Wageningen.

78 Ibid.

79 Raggs, *The Gospel of Barnabas*.

80 Slomp, *Islamochristiana*.

81 Ibid.

82 *Barnabas* uses the spelling 'Mohammed', but for the sake of consistency I have changed it to 'Muhammad'.

83 According to H. H. Scullard's article, 'Roman History' in *Encyclopaedia Britannica* (1973), the whole regular army of the Roman Empire at that time consisted of only 300,000 men!

84 Slomp, *Islamochristiana*.

85 For a fuller account of Wahb see Character 6.

86 Stern, *Journal of Theological Studies*.

87 Schonfield, Hugh J., *The Passover Plot* (London: Hutchinson, 1965).

88 Raggs, *The Gospel of Barnabas*.

Chapter Four

89 Jeffery, Graham, *The Gospel According to Barnabas* (Oxford: Mowbrays, 1975).

90 Al-Kitab, *The Gospel of Barnabas*.

91 Father Jacques Jomier in *Mélanges*, presented a long list of the historical and geographical errors he found in *Barnabas*. Among them were: Jesus was born when Pilate was governor; soldiers were not allowed in the temple; seven centres of hell are in agreement with the medieval seven kinds of sin; and Barnabas is made one of the twelve, and is as important as Peter is in the canonical Gospels (He is the fourth person present on the mount of transfiguration). Other points noted by Jomier are in the body of the text.

92 Toland, *Nazarenus*.

93 Cramer gives the feeling that an original was behind the manuscript he introduces.

94 Source for this information from *Preliminary Discourse*: Hughes, Thomas Patrick, *A Dictionary of Islam* (Clifton, New Jersey: Reference Book Publishers, 1965).

95 Nazir Ahmad, *Jesus in Heaven on Earth*.

96 Raggs, *The Gospel of Barnabas*.

97 Cirillo and Frémaux, *Évangile de Barnabé*.

98 Raggs, *The Gospel of Barnabas*.

99 The article is reprinted in *Moslem World* (Samuel M. Zwemer, ed.), vol. XIII (1923), Missionary Review Publishing Co. New York. The name of the editor of the *Epiphany* article is unknown.

100 Ragg, *Journal of Theological Studies*.

101 Baron Hubner in the shortened version of his *The Life and Times of Sixtus the Fifth*, translated by James F. Meline (New York: Catholic Publication Society, 1873), gives a view of Leti's writing style. His portrait of Sixtus is 'very fanciful'. He is presented as a 'pig-driver as a child; later a giddy and youthful monk; a restless and insupportable and ambitious subordinate; a facetious talker; a fanatical inquisitor; a hypocritical cardinal who threw away his crutches as soon as he had secured his election by a vulgar artifice ... a tyrannical pope ... Leti strove to make of Felice Peretti a cunning adventurer seeking through discreditable means to attain the object of his ambition'.

102 Von Pastor, Ludwig Freiherr, *Sixtus V*, vol. XXI of *The History of the Popes*, ed. Kerr, Ralph (London: Routledge & Kegan Paul, 1952).
103 Grendler, *The Roman Inquisition*.
104 Ibid.
105 Ibid.
106 Ibid.
107 Von Pastor, *Sixtus V*.
108 Hubner, *Sixtus V*.
109 Grendler, *The Roman Inquisition*.
110 Ibid.
111 Burton, Ivor Flower, 'Sixtus V' in *Encyclopaedia Britannica*, 1969 edition.
112 A story given by Von Pastor says this very well (Rome, Lent 1552): 'Half of Lent was passed, and Fra Felice [Peretti] was preparing himself for his sermon, when a fellow religious brought him a sealed letter which he had found in the pulpit of the Church of the Holy Apostles. Both of them thought it was a case of some request which it is customary to recommend to the hearers in the course of a sermon, and Fra Felice told his companion to place it with the other letters of the same kind. When, during the interval which as usual was made after the first part of the sermon, he opened it, he found that it was very far from being a request for prayers. On the contrary, on the sheet were written all the doctrines of the Catholic faith which Fra Felice had so far dealt with in his sermons, and against each was written the words: "Thou liest". In spite of his amazement, Fra Felice kept calm as he read it; it was only when he sought to hide the letter in his habit that many persons thought they detected certain signs of embarrassment. He hastened to end his sermon, and then sent the letter to the commissary-general of the Roman Inquisition, Michele Ghislieri. In his burning zeal, the latter at once went to see Fra Felice. When he was Pope, Sixtus V often used to speak of the terror he experienced, although he knew himself to be perfectly innocent, when this man entered his cell, with his severe countenance, his frowning expression and his deep set eyes. Ghislieri at once questioned him in short and grave words. But what appeared was not only the innocence of Felice, but also his zeal for the Catholic faith. Ghislieri's severe look vanished, and his whole appearance was changed, so that he seems to have become quite another man. With tears of joy he embraced the good Franciscan. Thenceforth the two men were closely associated.'
113 Raggs, *The Gospel of Barnabas*.
114 Brown, Horatio, *Studies in the History of Venice*, vol. II (London: John Murray, 1907).
115 Grendler, *The Roman Inquisition*.
116 Listed as SU, Bu.12, Padre Marin da Venezia; ASV: Archivo di Stato.

117 Chojnacki, Stanley, in private correspondence.
118 Grendler, *The Roman Inquisition*.
119 Ibid.
120 Ibid.
121 Su, Bu. 12, ASV.
122 Grendler, *The Roman Inquisition*.
123 Ludwig Von Pastor's *The History of the Popes* (vols. X–XVI) has useful and scattered references to Vergerio. Also useful is *Dictionnaire de Biographie Chrétienne et Anti-Chrétienne* (Paris: L'Abbé Migne, Aux Ateliers Catholiques, 1851).
124 Von Pastor, *The History of the Popes*.
125 Slomp, *Al-Mushir*.
126 Ibid.
127 Slomp, *Islamochristiana*.
128 Ibid.
129 Ibid.
130 The Raggs note: 'The Spanish version is described by Sale as a "moderate quarto"; the Italian as an octavo. The Spanish numbers 222 chapters, the Italian the same; the Spanish has 420 pages, the Italian – apart from the Dedication – 229 leaves, i.e. 458 pages'.
131 In his *Islamochristiana* article, Slomp says: 'Cirillo's assumption that the Spanish ms could not have been translated from the extant Italian ms because the preface in the [Vienna document] is missing, is not convincing. The preface to the Spanish text could very well have been written for that translation only. A second reason why they [Cirillo and Frémaux] believe a second Italian text did exist, which was probably the common ancestor of the present [*Barnabas*] and the Spanish fragment, are the differences between the two texts. But these differences are so minor they could easily be explained by personal freedom of the translator.'

Cirillo also postulated that *Barnabas* 'contains traces of a primitive text, probably the primitive gospel placed under the name and authority of the apostle Barnabas.' As Slomp continues his presentation of Cirillo's argument: 'Cirillo postulates ... an older gospel narrative which he thinks, was used by the medieval writer. This "narrative", which he calls "*écrit de base*" or "basic script" had probably the form of an "apology for Islam". This "defence of Islam" had incorporated a primitive Jewish–Christian source. It is no longer possible to find out in which language this older text must have been written. But Dr Cirillo believes that he can show the existence of "intermediary chains" between the author who placed the gospel ... under the name of Barnabas and the late Western medieval writer.'
132 Fletcher, *Novum Testamentum*.
133 The manuscript is incomplete. Chapter 120 ends on page 116, with a note that Chapters 121 to 200 are 'wanting'. It has yet to be fully

translated, and a comparison of the text with the Vienna document will probably shed further light on the authorship question.

134 Slomp, *Islamochristiana*.
135 Hubner, *Sixtus V*.
136 Jomier, *Mélanges*.
137 Cohn, Norman, 'Three Forgeries', *Encounter*, vol. XLIV, no. 1 (1975).
138 Slomp, *Islamochristiana*.

Chapter Five

139 *The Fundamentals* no author/editor (Los Angeles: Los Angeles Bible Institute, 1909).
140 John A. T. Robinson in *Redating the New Testament* (London: SCM, 1976) indicated that all twenty-seven New Testament books were produced in approximately the two decades before AD 70. He considered much of the accepted dating (typified by German critic Werner Kümmel's 1963 listing) to be the result of 'unexamined assumptions'. Robinson places John and Matthew at a much earlier time, *c*. AD 40–60. Mark comes a bit later, *c*. AD 45–60, and Luke–Acts at *c*. AD 55–65.
141 Lawrence, Jerome and Lee, Robert E., *Inherit the Wind* (New York: Bantam, 1969). The experience of the trial was devasting for Bryan; he died five days after the close. Scopes was convicted and fined $100. The defence appealed the case to the Tennessee Supreme Court which in 1927 upheld the constitutionality of the 1925 law, but cleared Scopes on the grounds that the lower court had exceeded its authority in fining Scopes the said amount.
142 Schonfield, *The Passover Plot*. 'God is Dead' was a fashionable theological term in the 1960s. Hick, John (ed.) *The Myth of God Incarnate* (London: SCM, 1977).
143 Guillaume, Alfred, *Islam* (Harmondsworth: Penguin, 1982). This is a good introduction into Islamic thought and background.
144 Mortimer, Edward, *Faith and Power: The Politics of Islam* (London: Faber, 1982).
145 Gibb, Hamilton, *Mohammedanism* (London: Oxford University Press, 1969). This has been re-issued with the title *Islam*. Gibb's book covers areas still neglected by more recent publications.
146 Arkoun, Muhammad, *Lectures du Coran* (Paris: Maisonneuve and Larouse, 1983).
147 Lewis, Bernard, 'The Revolt of Islam', in *New York Review of Books*, New York, 30 June 1983.
148 Darsh, S. M., *Muslims in Europe* (London, Ta-Ha, 1980).
149 Cragg, Kenneth, *The Call of the Minaret* (London: Oxford University Press, 1956).
150 Gibb, *Mohammedanism*.

151 Arberry, A. J., *The Koran Interpreted* (London: George Allen & Unwin, 1955).

152–157 Discussion of these authors in English can be found in Rabin, Chaim, *Qumran Studies* (London: Oxford University Press, 1957; New York: Schocken, 1975).

158 Ibid.

159 Ibid.

160 Muller, Herbert J., *The Loom of History* (New York: Harper & Row, 1958).

161 Parrinder, *Jesus in the Qur'an*.

162 Bowman, *Nederlands Theologisch Tijdschrift*.

163 Watt, W. Montgomery, *Muhammad at Mecca* (Oxford: Clarendon, 1953).

164 Andrae, Tor, *Mohammed* (London: George Allen & Unwin, 1936). Andrae's work is a little marred by psychological jargon, but his basic pursuit remains an incisive exploration into possible influences upon the development of Muhammad's thought.

165 Ibid.

166 Ibid.

167 Cragg, *The Call of the Minaret*.

168 Andrae, *Mohammed*.

169 Nazir Ahmad, *Jesus in Heaven on Earth*.

170 Bevan, A. A., 'Manichaeism', *Hastings Encyclopaedia of Religion and Ethics* (Edinburgh: Clark, 1926). Geo Widengren's *Mani and Manichaeism* (London: Weidenfeld & Nicolson, 1965) is useful on this point, and as a competent introduction to Mani's religious system.

171 Lady Drower's *The Mandaeans of Iraq and Iran* (Leiden: Brill, 1937; reissued 1962) remains the definitive work on the sect. I tried several years ago to initiate interest in the plight of the Mandaeans in Iraq and Iran due to the effects of the war fought in the area of their ancient homeland, and was disappointed that no one seemed very willing to take up their cause. An article was published, however, in the King's College, University of London *Theological Review* (Sox, 'The Last of the Gnostics', vol. VI, no. 2, 1983). It is sad that they no longer possess any champions like Lady Drower, and almost scandalous that the major scholarly interest expressed is tainted by arguments concerning their relationship to the existence of a pre-Christian Gnosticism, or not. A notable exception to this has been the admirable notice given them by Kurt Rudolph.

172 Lady Drower's account of the 'exodus' from the *Haran Gawaitha* 'tells of a persecution of Nasoraeans in the first century AD by Jews in Jerusalem and describes the flight of a number of the sect to Harran where, amongst the Parthians they found [Jewish?] gnostics like themselves'.

173 Bell, Richard, *Origin of Islam in its Christian Environment* (London: Cass, 1968) a reissue of the Gunning Lectures at Edinburgh University, 1925.

174 Blunt, *The Acts of the Apostles.*
175 Segelberg, Eric, 'Zidqa Brika and the Mandaean Problem', *Proceedings of the International Colloquium on Gnosticism, 1973.* Segelberg raised a few points about Mani's background due to the discovery of a tiny fifth-century Greek Manichaean codex (called the Cologne Codex). The translation of an early Syriac text seemed to indicate that Mani belonged not to a Mandaean community but to the Elkesaites.
176 Simon, *Jewish Sects.*
177 For references on the Elkesaites see: Brandt, W. 'Elchasai', *Ein Religionsstifter und sein Werk* (Leiden: Brill, 1912), and Andrae, *Mohammed.*
178 Rudolph, Kurt, *Mandaism* (Leiden: Brill, 1978).
179 See Yamauchi, Edwin, *Pre-Christian Gnosticism* (Grand Rapids, Michigan: Eerdmans, 1973).
180 Wansbrough, John, *The Sectarian Milieu* (London: Oxford University Press, 1978). It should be noted that Rabin himself admits that his analysis 'may appear fanciful from the outset'.
181 Tibawi, A. L. *Second Critique of English-Speaking Orientalists and Their Approach to Islam and the Arabs* (London: Islamic Cultural Centre, 1979).
182 Guillaume, *Islam.*
183 Macuch, Rudolf, 'Gnostische Ethik und die Anfange der Mandaer', *Christentum am Rotem* (Berlin: F. Altheim and R. Stiehl, 1973).
184 *The Nazarene Gospel Restored,* mentioned by Robinson, John A. T., *Can We Trust the New Testament?* (London: Mowbray, 1977); Allegro, John, *The Sacred Mushroom and the Cross* (London: Hodder & Stoughton, 1970); Baigent, M., Leigh, R. and Lincoln, H., *The Holy Blood and the Holy Grail* (London: Jonathan Cape, 1982).
185 As quoted in *Newsweek,* 24 December 1979.
186 Zaehner, R. C. *At Sundry Times* (London: Faber, 1958).

Chapter Six

187 Brownrigg, Ronald, *The Twelve Apostles* (London: Weidenfeld & Nicolson, 1974).
188 Baidawi's commentary is mentioned in Parrinder, *Jesus in the Qur'an.*
189 Dimaski's commentary is mentioned in the article, 'Judas Iscariot' in *The New Encyclopaedia Britannica,* vol. V (Chicago: Encyclopaedia Britannica Inc., 1982).
190 Stern, *Journal of Theological Studies.*
191 Ibid. Arthur Jeffery in *A Reader on Islam* (London: Weidenfeld & Nicolson, 1974) gives the account from 'A Prophet's Story', the story of Jesus in *Qisas al-Anbiya* of Abu Ishaq Ahmad ath-Thalabi (eleventh century): 'they spat on him and put thorns upon him, and

147

they set up a wooden stake on which to crucify him. When they came with him to the stake the earth was darkened, and Allah sent angels who came between them and Jesus. Then he cast the appearance of Jesus upon him who had led them to him, whose name was Judas, so they crucified him in his place, thinking he was Jesus'.

192   Ibid.
193   Ibid.
194   Ibid.
195   Ibid.
196   *The Nag Hammadi Library*, Robinson, James M., gen. ed. (New York: Harper & Row, 1981).
197   Hussein, M. K. Hasayn, *City of Wrong: A Friday in Jerusalem*, translated by Cragg, Kenneth (London: Bles, 1959).
198   Hourani, *Europe and the Middle East*.
199   Hussein, *City of Wrong*.
200   Ibid.
201   Dawood, *The Koran*.
202   Zaehner, *At Sundry Times*.
203   Elder, E. E., 'Crucifixion of Jesus in the Koran', *Moslem World* (Samuel M. Zwemer, ed.), vol. XIII (1923), Missionary Review Publishing Co., New York.
204   Basetti-Sani, Giulio, *The Koran in the Light of Christ: A Christian Interpretation of the Sacred Book of Islam* (Chicago: Franciscan Herald, 1977).
205   Ibid.
206   Darsh, *Muslims in Europe*.
207   Atta Jalandhri, Abul, *Death on the Cross?* (London: London Mosque, 1976).
208   Cragg, *The Call of the Minaret*.

Chapter Seven

209   Schweitzer, Albert, *The Quest for the Historical Jesus, A Critical Study of Its Progress from Reimarus to Wrede*, translated by Montgomery, W. (London: A. & C. Black, 1910).
210   Albert Hourani, in *Europe and the Middle East*, relates: 'In a famous lecture [Carlyle] depicts Muhammad as an example of a type of mind which has appeared again and again in human history, the "prophetic" type. The prophet is a certain kind of human hero who carries certain human qualities to the limit: "a silent great soul ... one of those who cannot *but* be in earnest": austere, intuitive, looking "through the show of things into *things*", convinced and propagating Islam through conviction not through the sword, and above all sincere. Whether he was in fact inspired by God is not to be known: perhaps Carlyle himself has doubts of it'.
211   Dawood, *The Koran*, 19.17–38.

212   Hayek, P. (*Le Christ de L'Islam*, Paris, 1959) quoted in G. C. Anawati's article, 'Isa' in the Encyclopaedia of Islam, new edition (Leiden: Brill, 1971).

213   Zaehner, *At Sundry Times*.

214   *The Lost Books of the Bible*, no editor/author (New York: New American Library, 1974). This is a very mixed collection, but contains full accounts of many examples of New Testament Apocrypha. The sycamore tree at Matrarieh (Matarea), Heliopolis, is one of the four sites of the flight into Egypt venerated by Muslims and Christians.

215   James, *The Apocryphal New Testament*.

216   Hennecke, *New Testament Apocrypha*.

217   Parrinder, *Jesus in the Qur'an*.

218   Anawati, *Encyclopaedia of Islam*.

219   Ashraf, *The Prophets*.

220   Vermes, Geza, *Jesus the Jew: A Historian's Reading of the Gospels* (London: Collins, 1973; Fontana, 1976).

221   Cullman, Oscar, *Christology of the New Testament* (Philadelphia: Westminster, 1959).

222   Dawood, *The Koran*, 5.110–117.

223   Mingana, A., 'Syriac Influence on the Style of the Kur'an', *The Bulletin of the John Rylands Library*, vol. II, no. 1 (January 1927).

224   Parrinder, *Jesus in the Qur'an*.

225   Ibid.

226   Hennecke, *New Testament Apocrypha*.

227   Ashraf, *The Prophets*.

228   Mufassir, Sulayman Shahid, 'Who Is the "Paraclete"?', *Impact* (28 December 1973-10 January 1974), London.

229   Watt, *Muhammad at Mecca*.

230   Schacht, J., 'Ahmad', *Encyclopaedia of Islam*, new edition (Leiden: Brill, 1960).

231   Anawati, *Encyclopaedia of Islam*.

232   Goldziher, Ignaz, *Introduction to Islamic Theology and Law*, trans. A. and R. Hamori (Princeton, New Jersey: Princeton University Press, 1981).

233   Parrinder, *Jesus in the Qur'an*.

234   Ashraf, *The Prophets*.

235   Nasr, Seyyed Hossein, *Ideals and Realities of Islam* (London: George Allen & Unwin, 1966).

236   Ibid.

237   Hart, Michael H., *The 100: A Ranking of the Most Influential Persons in History* (New York: Galahad, 1978). Hart explains his choice of Muhammad: 'my ranking Muhammad higher than Jesus ... because of my belief that Muhammad had a much greater personal influence on the formulation of the Muslim religion than Jesus had on the formulation of the Christian religion ... There is no question that

Christianity, over the course of time, has had far more adherents than any other religion ... [but] Christianity, unlike Islam, was not founded by a single person but by two people – Jesus and St. Paul – and the principal credit for its development must therefore be apportioned between those two figures'.

238 Kateregga, Badru D., and Shenk, David W., *Islam and Christianity: A Muslim and a Christian in Dialogue* (Grand Rapids, Michigan: Eerdmans, 1980).

Chapter Eight

239 Hugh-Jones, Stephen, *The Economist*, 25 December 1982.
240 Guillaume, *Islam*. It might be noted that using the Nicene Creed would see fewer agreements.
241 Hourani, *Europe and the Middle East*.
242 Poole-Connor, E. J., *Mohammedanism: What Is It?* (London: Fellowship of Faith for the Muslims, no date).
243 The booklet includes a list of 'delicate subjects' of which the missionary must be aware.
244 *The Sunday Times*, 20 March 1983, had this brief article: '*Moslem Convert*: Roger Garaudy, former leader of the French Communist Party, has just pilgrimaged to Mecca to obtain the title of Hajii. Garaudy, who ran for president of France in 1981, began as a militant Protestant. In the late sixties he left the Party and became a Catholic. On Monday the new convert was guest of honour at a reception by the Sheik of al-Azhar. The sheik, praying for Garaudy, gave him a reason for at last remaining faithful. Moslems who abandon their faith are automatically sentenced to death in all 41 Islamic countries.'
245 Hugh-Jones, *The Economist*.
246 Mertens, Victor, *The New Vitality of Islam in Black Africa and Its Pastoral Implications* (Konigstein: Kirche in Not/Ostpriesterhilfe, 1980).
247 I am considering a broad century before the Protestant Reformation.
248 Islam's source remains basically the same, with increased importance in Africa and Indonesia.
249 Naipaul, V. S., *Among the Believers: An Islamic Journey* (New York: Knopf, 1981).
250 Official reports which use the term describe the process as a matter of defending and protecting Islamic values and cultural traditions against Western influences.
251 Hourani, *Europe and the Middle East*.
252 Ibid.
253 The Church of Jesus Christ of the Latter-Day Saints, which based itself on the revelation to Smith, the *Book of Mormon*, is one of the few successful new religious systems of modern times.

254 Mertens, *The New Vitality of Islam*.
255 Coonan, John L., *Islam Comes To Britain* (London: Catholic Truth Society, 1979).
256 There are a large number of these tracts, including: *The Sources of Christianity* by Al-Hajj Khwaja Kamal-Ud-Din; *Fundamentals of the Christian Faith in the Light of the Gospels* by Ahmadiyyah Anjuman Isha'at Islam; *Islam and Christianity* by Mrs Ulfat Aziz-Us-Samad; and *A Talk between a Muslim and a Christian* by Fazl Ilahi Anweri. Most of them are available from Ahmadiyyah Anjuman Isha'at-I-Islam, Ahmadiyyah Buildings, Brandeth Road, Lahore 7, Pakistan.
257 On 23 May 1983, President Reagan brought the attention of the world to the plight of the Baha'is in Iran by asking for the release of twenty-two of their leaders sentenced to death for spying. The Baha'i faith is considered a Muslim heresy in Iran, the country of its origin. It was founded in 1863, and considers Abraham, Moses, Jesus, Muhammad and the Bab (who prophesised the coming of a great world Teacher, Baha'ullah) as revealers of God's one truth. The movement stresses the unity of religious systems, and is said to have 400,000 members in Iran.
258 Jansen, G. H., *Militant Islam* (New York: Harper & Row, 1979).
259 El-Droubie, Riadh, 'A Muslim Looks at Christianity and the Church', *The Minaret*, vol. 2, no. 1 (January–March 1978).
260 Hugh-Jones, *The Economist*.
261 *The Tablet*, 22 January 1983.
262 Coonan, *Islam Comes to Britain*.
263 Aguilar, *Islamochristiana*.
264 Mertens, *The New Vitality of Islam*.
265 Slomp, *Al-Mushir*.
266 Basetti-Sani, *The Koran in the Light of Christ*.
267 One worth noting is *The Holy War Jihad: The Destiny of the Moslem World* by the evangelist Lester Sumrall (South Bend, Indiana: Lesea, 1980). Sumrall urges his radio audiences: 'Let's win a million Persians to Christ in our time'.
268 Baar, Marius, *The Unholy War* (Worthing: Henry Walter, 1980).
269 Ibid.
270 Ibid.
271 Christian fundamentalists have a variety of beliefs concerning the 'end times'. Some believe in some form of millennialism. The 'millennium' is a prophesied thousand-year period of events on the earth surrounding the Second Coming of Jesus. Pre-millennialists believe Jesus will come before the millennium, to reign for a thousand years, finally defeat all the forces of evil, and claim the world for God. Post-millennialists believe that Jesus will come to reign after the thousand-year period of seeing the gospel finally conquer the world. Some say that seven years before the millennium the last trumpet will sound and all the saved will instantly be caught

151

up into heaven. Two major happenings will follow: the gospel will be preached (by believing Jews since all Christians have departed), and Israel will be converted. The second event is the rise of the Antichrist, who will attack Israel. After the defeat of the Antichrist, Jesus will come down to establish his earthly throne at Jerusalem. The foregoing was adapted from Hadden, Jeffrey K. and Swann, Charles E., *Prime Time Preachers* (Reading, Massachusetts: Addison-Wesley, 1981).

272 A worthwhile article in this connection is Robert Faricy's 'Via Dolorosa', *The Tablet*, 2–9 April 1983.

273 Slomp, *Al-Mushir*.